Studies of the Americas

Series Editor
Maxine Molyneux
Institute of the Americas
University College London
London, UK

The Studies of the Americas Series includes country specific, cross-disciplinary and comparative research on the United States, Latin America, the Caribbean, and Canada, particularly in the areas of Politics, Economics, History, Anthropology, Sociology, Anthropology, Development, Gender, Social Policy and the Environment. The series publishes monographs, readers on specific themes and also welcomes proposals for edited collections, that allow exploration of a topic from several different disciplinary angles. This series is published in conjunction with University College London's Institute of the Americas under the editorship of Professor Maxine Molyneux.

More information about this series at
http://www.palgrave.com/gp/series/14462

Claire Lindsay

Magazines, Tourism, and Nation-Building in Mexico

Claire Lindsay
Department of Spanish, Portuguese,
   and Latin American Studies
University College London
London, UK

Studies of the Americas
ISBN 978-3-030-01002-7   ISBN 978-3-030-01003-4 (eBook)
https://doi.org/10.1007/978-3-030-01003-4

Library of Congress Control Number: 2018957069

© The Editor(s) (if applicable) and The Author(s) 2019. This book is an open access publication.
Open Access This book is licensed under the terms of the Creative Commons Attribution 4.0 International License (http://creativecommons.org/licenses/by/4.0/), which permits use, sharing, adaptation, distribution and reproduction in any medium or format, as long as you give appropriate credit to the original author(s) and the source, provide a link to the Creative Commons license and indicate if changes were made.
The images or other third party material in this book are included in the book's Creative Commons license, unless indicated otherwise in a credit line to the material. If material is not included in the book's Creative Commons license and your intended use is not permitted by statutory regulation or exceeds the permitted use, you will need to obtain permission directly from the copyright holder.
The use of general descriptive names, registered names, trademarks, service marks, etc. in this publication does not imply, even in the absence of a specific statement, that such names are exempt from the relevant protective laws and regulations and therefore free for general use.
The publisher, the authors and the editors are safe to assume that the advice and information in this book are believed to be true and accurate at the date of publication. Neither the publisher nor the authors or the editors give a warranty, express or implied, with respect to the material contained herein or for any errors or omissions that may have been made. The publisher remains neutral with regard to jurisdictional claims in published maps and institutional affiliations.

Cover illustration: © Melisa Hasan

This Palgrave Pivot imprint is published by the registered company Springer Nature Switzerland AG
The registered company address is: Gewerbestrasse 11, 6330 Cham, Switzerland

In memory of Andrea Noble

Acknowledgements

There are many people who have assisted me in writing this book in different ways, whether by listening to my ideas and sharing theirs, reading and commenting on early drafts, inviting me to give papers at seminars or conferences, asking pertinent questions, recommending reading, writing references for related grant applications, or simply providing valuable encouragement when it was most needed (and appreciated). My thanks to all: Lucy Bell, Zoltán Biedermann, Stephanie Bird, María del Pilar Blanco, Felipe Botelho Correa, Catherine Boyle, Matthew Brown, Elizabeth Chant, Eleanor Chiari, Jo Crow, Maria Chiara D'Argenio, Charles Forsdick, Guadalupe Gerardi, Katherine Ibbett, Ed King, John King, Julia Kuehn, Lorraine Leu, Angela Lindsay, Roger Lindsay, Sylvia Molloy, Maxine Molyneux, Andrea Noble, Joanna Page, Thomas Rath, Lauren Rea, Luis Rebaza Soraluz, Elisa Sampson Tudela, Erica Segre, Paul Smethurst, Ana Suriani da Silva, Camilla Sutherland, Philip Swanson, Alia Trabucco, Maite Usoz de la Fuente, Ann Varley, David Wood, Gareth Wood, and Tim Youngs. I am thankful for the editorial work of Anca Pusca and Katelyn Zingg and to the three anonymous readers at Palgrave. And I couldn't have done anything at all without dearest Mark and Fabian, who loves maps and has already come so far.

I am grateful for the assistance of staff at the Bancroft Library, University of California, Berkeley, the Harry Ransom Center and the Nettie Lee Benson Latin American Collection at University of Texas, Austin. I am particularly grateful for the award of a Harry Ransom Center research fellowship which enabled access to Anita Brenner's papers; for a UCL-Santander Research Catalyst award and to the British Academy, which both funded research visits to the United States and Mexico. University College London's progressive policy of granting a term's research leave following parental leave was also essential in bringing work that had been conducted over several years to completion in the autumn of 2017.

Parts of Chapter 4 were published in my essay 'Map Reading in Travel Writing: the Explorers' Maps of *Mexico This Month*' in *New Directions in Travel Writing Studies*, edited by Julia Kuehn and Paul Smethurst (Palgrave Macmillan, 2015), pp. 199–212, reproduced with permission of Palgrave Macmillan.

Contents

1 Introduction — 1

2 Tourism, Nation-Building, and Magazines — 17

3 Tourism Advertisements in *Mexican Folkways* (1925–1937) — 53

4 Mapping Capital in *Mexico This Month* (1955–1971) — 91

5 Conclusion — 127

Index — 137

List of Figures

Fig. 2.1	Front cover of *Mexico This Month*, 3:1, 1957	33
Fig. 2.2	Advertisements in *Mexican Folkways*, 4:1, 1928	35
Fig. 3.1	Front cover of *Mexican Folkways*, 5:1, 1929	59
Fig. 3.2	Elegantes advertisement, *Mexican Folkways*, 3, 1927	67
Fig. 3.3	Número 12 advertisement, *Mexican Folkways*	68
Fig. 3.4	Hotel Genève advertisement, *Mexican Folkways*, 3:1, 1927, p. 1	73
Fig. 3.5	Hotel Genève advertisement, *Mexican Folkways*, 9:1, 1937, p. 1	74
Fig. 4.1	Explorer's map of La Lagunilla market, *Mexico This Month*, 1:9, 1955	106
Fig. 4.2	Explorer's map of the main drag in Mexico city, via the Paseo de la Reforma, *Mexico This Month*, 4:9, 1958	108
Fig. 4.3	Map of Chapultepec Woods, *Mexico This Month*, 2:1, 1956	109
Fig. 4.4	Trail of Cortés, a map for intrepid explorers, *Mexico This Month*, 3:8, 1957	111
Fig. 4.5	Wayward Wanderers' map of Oaxaca, *Mexico This Month*, 3:10, 1957	112
Fig. 4.6	The Complete Explorers' map for Treasure Hunters on Land and Sea, *Mexico This Month*, 3:11, 1957	114
Fig. 5.1	Reader's letter, *Mexico This Month*	130

CHAPTER 1

Introduction

Abstract This chapter, drawing first on pertinent archival material from Anita Brenner's papers, introduces the book's main concerns in brief—the relation between print culture, tourism, and nationhood, and the (geo)political ramifications of content and style in and beyond the periodical's pages—before elucidating its overall scope, shape, and principal objectives. It provides a theoretical rationale for the study (referring to the work of Néstor García Canclini and Benedict Anderson as well as reinterpretations of the latter's ideas within Latin American cultural studies) and ends with an overview of the main chapters.

Keywords Tourism · Magazines · Nationhood · Mexico · United States · Diplomacy · Visual culture

> *Mexico was not so much a place as a journey that required no travel.*
> Carrera (2011: 108)

Anita Brenner's 1947 article for the magazine *Holiday* is a signature blend of evocative description and touristic information about places of interest in Mexico, with historical and ethnographic details about its colonial past, fiestas, and present-day society. The feature begins with one of Brenner's favourite metaphors, and a trope to which she returned throughout her career: the journey south across the border is a passage 'through the looking glass ... into never-never land', which is not only 'another world, as tantalizing and disturbing as a dream' but 'a place that shakes you like a mental atom-splitter and cuts you loose like a balloon' (1947a: 2). That arresting image lays the groundwork for Brenner's articulation of Mexico's 'fundamental characteristic ... that it is an Indian country' (1947a: 46). Indeed, as part of her ethnographic survey, Brenner criticizes the hypocrisy of Mexican elites who, in order to identify as 'American', at once exploit and/or disavow the country's indigenous peoples while they repudiate its poverty and corruption. She also mocks a figure she elsewhere calls the 'Typical Tourist', who, when following the tourist circuit, 'get[s] a Mexico served up anxiously in the gringo image; as interpreted by knowing promoters and hopeful catchers-of-crumbs' (1932: n.p.).[1] In *Holiday* Brenner acknowledges, in the twenty-five or so years since the Revolution, the opacity of Mexican politics, the country's enduring inequalities of wealth and land distribution, its high illiteracy rates, poverty, and poor sanitation: that Mexico is a place that can be 'exasperating, baffling, and shocking'. Yet she insists on its commitment to democracy and that it is 'a country in transition ... trying to cover a lot of ground very fast'. Above all, she identifies in Mexico a critical quality then absent in the United States and which she avows would lure thousands of tourists to its shores: 'that sweet, sweet personal sense of freedom' (1947a: 61, 62, 63).

The *Holiday* article was just one of Brenner's prolific writings on travel to Mexico, which, together with her authorship of the guidebook *Your Mexican Holiday* (1932), included contributions to English-language magazines and newspapers in the United States, such as *Atlantic Monthly*, *Fortune*, *Mademoiselle*, *The Nation*, *New York Evening Post*, and *The New York Times Sunday Magazine*.[2] This piece, however, became notorious and was reprinted over several weeks as a column in the Mexican national daily *Excelsior*. The newspaper issued a cautionary prefatory note to the article's serialization in 'Realidad y ficción en México': '*Excelsior*, que no se hace solidario de los conceptos de la autora, ha querido, sin embargo, divulgar el presente artículo para que los lectores vean como se nos juzga en el extranjero y para que los juicios que contiene lleguen a conocimiento de las personas que quisieran refutarlos' [*Excelsior*, which does not sympathize with the author's position, nonetheless wants to publish the following article so that readers can see how they view us abroad and so that the opinions it contains come to the attention of those who would like to challenge them]

(Brenner, n.d.). Against the newspaper's charges that her unpromising picture of Mexico had frightened tourists away, Brenner, in private correspondence with the editor (and not for the last time in her travel/writing career), defended her use of figurative language:

> la intencion irónica de estas frases [sobre los extranjeros en Mexico] es tan evidente que no creo yo se le puede escapar a nadie ... Sin embargo, el artículo recalca, antes y después de esas observaciones, que mucho de lo que se cuenta al turista de lo que le asusta, es leyenda. (Brenner 1947b)

> [the ironic intention of those words (about foreigners in Mexico) is so obvious it couldn't escape anyone's attention, in my view ... However, the article emphasizes throughout that much of what frightens the tourist is simply fiction]

Brenner was also robust about the ethics of her piece, insisting that it was poverty and poor sanitation that alarmed tourists, not information about or historical contextualization of said conditions. Tourists, Brenner contended, 'gozan de la voluntad y la habilidad de comprender' [have the desire and ability to understand]: meanwhile, the disservice done to Mexico was not that she had written about those issues but rather 'la poquedad de espíritu de aquellos mexicanos que se espantan tanto de lo suyo, que todo lo quisieran esconder detrás de imitaciones y fandangos' [the meanness of spirit of those Mexicans who are so frightened of aspects of their own country that they want to hide them all behind imitations and fandangos] (Brenner 1947b).

In addition to the adverse coverage it received in the Mexican press, Brenner's *Holiday* feature provoked a charged exchange of letters between Mexico's then Minister for Tourism, Alejandro Buelna, and Brenner's agent, Guillermo Hawley, in what became tantamount to a diplomatic dispute. Buelna took umbrage at Brenner's audacity as 'a foreigner living here and enjoying our hospitality to go to the lengths that [she] did' (Brenner 1947c). Despite her 'admirable' reputation, Buelna accused Brenner of 'twisting half truths with whole truths around in such a manner ... that confuse[s] the average reader' (Brenner 1947c). What he called Brenner's 'anti-Christian, anti-Spanish, anti-upper caste' 'overvaluation' of Mexico's Indian peoples and heritage together with her inclusion of details about the country's inequities were features that would have contradicted the image of a modern Mexico that the state was then trying to project, promote, and protect internationally.

Meanwhile, Hawley proposed to Buelna that his client's only miscalculation in the *Holiday* piece was to adopt such a sensationalist tone, although he observed that that was the prevailing cadence of US journalism: 'we probably need a writer like Anita to wake us to the realization that all is not rosy in the tourist business,' he suggested, 'and that a number of serious situations require correcting' (Brenner 1947d).

I begin with this incident in detail because it provides a striking distillation of some of the principal themes of this study of magazines, tourism, and nation-building in modern Mexico. First, the *Holiday* feature is an exemplary expression of Brenner's tireless advocacy of the culture of and commitment to tourism in Mexico, which would define her career as a writer and editor. It synthesizes the proclivities of content and style that underpinned the editorial work on *Mexico This Month*, which, like *Mexican Folkways*, the other of two magazines this book considers, aimed to disseminate information about Mexico's culture to audiences north and south of the Mexico–US border. Second, the ensuing debacle about the *Holiday* feature spotlights the acute sensitivities of the Mexican state to what it perceived as deleterious images of the country in the foreign press during the post-revolutionary period, sensitivities that have long since endured and resurfaced at different junctures. It also speaks to the transnational reach and power of the periodical press, a cultural form to which the Mexican state itself turned from the 1920s onwards in order to boost tourism.[3] Third, Brenner's defence of her *Holiday* contribution to *Excelsior*, significantly, rests on legitimacy and raises broader questions of national and cultural authenticity, values that are at the heart of the experience and narration of tourism more generally. Taking up the issue of national elites' sense of shame about Mexico, Brenner, who held US citizenship, advocates 'orgullo de lo que se es' [pride in what you are]: 'Siendo yo nacida en México e identificada toda mi vida y obra con este país, me creo con el derecho de ese orgullo' [Having been born in Mexico and identified all my life and work with this country, I believe I have the right to that pride] (Brenner 1947b). Her magazine and earlier writing for *Mexican Folkways* can be seen precisely in this affirmative guise, as a means of championing Mexico and its culture to an international audience. Moreover, Brenner's transnational affiliations, identifications, and networks are a defining feature of the period after Revolution in Mexico, when cross-border travel, residence, and (business, cultural, and scholarly) cooperation were common. They are too a distinguishing characteristic of the periodicals, *Mexican Folkways* and

Mexico This Month, under scrutiny in what follows, each of which was the fruit of transcultural collaborations that were politically endorsed and funded by the Mexican state and the like of which became especially well established in the cultural arena from the 1920s onwards.

As such, in addition to the North American magazine providing a 'prototype' of sorts for the periodical she would go on to edit in Mexico in years to come, the dispute over Brenner's *Holiday* article allows us to more fully contextualize and apprehend the later editorial policy, design, and fate of her own and other magazines of the period. As discussed in Chapter 3, one of the principal objectives of *Mexico This Month* became the contestation and correction of disadvantageous views of Mexico circulating in the US press—the very kind of 'wrongdoing' of which Brenner had been accused by Buelna in the *Holiday* feature. In turn, the aims of *Mexican Folkways*, edited by Frances Toor, a magazine to which Brenner contributed earlier in her career (and which is the subject of Chapter 2), were to record and communicate the customs and traditions of Mexico's indigenous peoples just as they were being reevaluated in anthropological debates and in developing conceptualizations of the country as a modern Republic. To this degree, the two magazines examined in this study shared political, even nationalistic ambitions, as well as personnel. In *Mexico This Month* the question of tone would once again be paramount, as it was in *Holiday*, with Brenner's trademark breezy editorial style constituting a significant (though, as we shall see, not entirely infallible) articulation of the former magazine's avowed ambassadorial objectives. Cadence was also a consideration in the aesthetic composition of the earlier *Mexican Folkways*, which in addition to documenting the country's folklore also comprised a catalogue of works by Mexico's foremost visual artists and photographers. In short, where the *Holiday* feature exhorted the kind of vicarious journey-making to Mexico to which this chapter's epigraph refers, the two periodicals at the heart of this study in different ways sought to galvanize (empirical and figurative) tourism in/to the new Republic as it emerged from Revolution and entered into twentieth-century global modernity. Like their North American counterpart, these magazines' publication and particular interventions into tourism had manifold political ramifications at national and international levels.

* * * *

This book is about the relation between periodicals, tourism, and nation-building in Mexico. It enquires into how magazines, a staple form of the promotional apparatus of tourism since its inception, articulated an imaginative geography of Mexico during a period in which that industry became a critical means of economic recovery and political stability after the Revolution. Neither magazines nor tourism were new to Mexico then: the picture supplements of nineteenth-century newspapers can be seen as forerunners of the contemporary periodical and organized tourism to the country dates back to at least the 1880s. Yet the period under scrutiny here is of crucial importance in terms of developments in print culture and the travel industry alike. For instance, in 1928, in the midst of its national reconstruction, the Mexican government passed legislation that officially launched its role in the regulation of tourism: among an array of commissions involved in organizing the industry (including the National Tourism Committee, CNT), a Pro-Tourism Commission (CPT) was formed to standardize entry for tourists at the US–Mexico border.[4] The intervention of Alberto Mascareñas, director general of the newly formed Bank of Mexico, who created a Department of Tourism in April 1928, was also decisive: the bank would go on to become a major sponsor of tourism development projects, including the completion of Mexico's first international highway from Nuevo Laredo to Monterrey. Thus, while it '[ought] to [have been] a kind of imperialism that …worked against revolutionary nationalism', at this time tourism, insofar as it helped shape national identity as Mexico established itself as a modern Republic, became 'compatible' with the goals of the Revolution (Berger 2006: 20, 3).[5]

During that same decade, numerous magazines emerged in and outside Mexico to become a popular and widely distributed form of documenting and disseminating the country's culture and creative currents. These included pedagogical titles (such as *El Maestro*, 1921–1923, and *El libro y el pueblo*, 1922–1970, both published by the Ministry of Education (Secretaría de Educación Pública or SEP); political or 'working class' titles, such as *El Machete* (1924) and *Revista Crom* (1925); and iterations of the so-called little or avant-garde magazines such as *Forma: Revista de artes plásticas* (1926–1928), *Horizonte* (1926–1927), *Ulises* (1928), *Contemporáneos* (1928–1931) and *Crisol* (1929–1934), among others. An important but hitherto overlooked subcategory of transnational magazine became a part of a raft of measures to stimulate tourism and refashion nationhood from this time onwards, as much to lure the tourist dollar south, as to counteract habitually prejudicial views of Mexico then circulating abroad. Such periodicals, deployed by both state and private actors from both sides of the border, who often worked in collaboration, included the Department of Tourism's inaugural English-language brochure of 1929, William Furlong's monthly newsletter about Mexico of the 1930s, brochures produced by the AMT (Asociación Mexicana de Turismo) before and after WWII, and titles such as *Mexican World: Voice of Latin America* and Howard Phillips's long-running *Mexican Life: Mexico's Monthly Review*, established in 1924. Those and the magazines under consideration in this book functioned as 'guides' to what they purported to be the 'real' Mexico to domestic and international readers alike. Notwithstanding their vogue, popularity, reach, and close affiliation to industry and state, such magazines have not received any sustained critical attention in the scholarship on tourism or nation-building in Mexico. This book aims to redress that oversight: it argues that magazines, in their responsive, serialized forms, and intrinsic aesthetic heterogeneity, offer a rich and compelling object of study in terms of both.

The book considers two salient case studies of such magazines, *Mexican Folkways* (1925–1937) and *Mexico This Month* (1955–1971), both of which were binational titles, public–private collaborations, produced and published in Mexico City. The well-known bilingual *Mexican Folkways*, in concert with contemporary ideas in anthropology and debates among nationalist elites, was the first magazine of its kind to describe 'customs … art, music, archaeology, and the Indian himself as part of the new social trends' in Mexico (7:4, 1932, 208). As Rick López writes, 'No other source did more during the late 20s and early 30s … to encourage an appreciation for the culture and arts of the Mexican countryside' (2010: 103). *Mexican Folkways* ardently promoted Mexico's contemporary visual culture too, through features on and reproductions of the work of artists such as José Clemente Orozco and its art editor Diego Rivera, who designed the magazine's distinctive front covers (see Fig. 3.1).

As such, its general editor Frances Toor claimed that *Folkways* had an 'important influence on the modern art movement' (7:4, 1932, 205). By the same token, the perhaps less familiar English-language magazine *Mexico This Month* was also a first of its kind, conceived as a vehicle of soft diplomacy, to broker neighbourly international relations between north and south. Launched under the auspices of a self-styled group of businessman called the Comité norteamericano pro-México, *Mexico This Month* aimed to improve social and business relations between Mexico and the United States by promoting travel, investment, and retirement in

Mexico. Its editor Anita Brenner, who served an informal apprenticeship under Toor as a contributor to *Folkways*, enlisted Mexican and North American writers and illustrators to express what she called 'Mexico's wealth of beauty in full colour' between the magazine's covers. Both periodicals, though they spoke in different ways to national cultural and political issues and debates, emerged from and responded to a particular urgency after the Revolution to explore and contribute to the consolidation of a new national consciousness: insofar as both were recipients of (albeit precarious sources of) state funding, to varying degrees they were also both implicated in what Carlos Monsiváis has called 'state control of the significance of being Mexican' (Hellier-Tinoco 2011: 57). Notwithstanding divergences in style, circulation, and outlook between *Mexican Folkways* and *Mexico This Month*, their 'nationalistic' and/or periodized titles speak to that shared impulse; to articulate what one editor boldly but disingenuously called 'no dogma ... beyond fidelity to Mexico' (Mraz 2009: 156). Since neither periodical has been digitized nor even previously (fully) read or studied, this book draws on the findings of archival research in order to provide the first account of these titles and their publication histories and to offer an original analysis of their role in an industry that has been fundamental to the formation of modern Mexico. In doing so, the book perceives these magazines as an essential but hitherto undervalued part of Mexico's 'culture of the visual' (Mirzoeff 2015: 11).

The visual forms of tourism's promotional arsenal create imaginative geographies that do more than simply reflect the ideologies of their authors/creators: they have frequently shaped and become a constitutive part of the very spaces they imagine. In this respect, this book is aligned with others in the fields of Mexican cultural history and tourism studies that are interested in the discursive construction of geography and space and in the connections between imagining and nation formation. Such interests typically rest on and extrapolate the now seminal work of Benedict Anderson on the nation as an 'imagined community', which, though it has not been received uncritically in Latin American studies and elsewhere, in its insistence on the association between print culture and nationalism and that nations are 'distinguished not by their falsity/ genuineness, but by the style in which they are imagined', remains pertinent (Anderson 2006: 7).[6] This book takes its cue from a number of (re)articulations of Anderson's proposal in the context of Latin America and its visual culture by scholars such as Mauricio Tenorio Trillo, Jens

Andermann, and Shelley Garrigan who have focused in different ways on the role of national elites in respect of exhibitions, museums, and monuments during the long and critical nineteenth century, in which nation-states were consolidating across the region. This was a time when in Mexico particularly, as Nestor García Canclini observes, 'the consecration and celebration of the patrimony, its knowledge and use, [was] basically a visual operation' (1995: 118). Tenorio Trillo, for example, in his work on Mexico at the world's fairs, 'underscore[s] the importance of form, style, façade' not as separate to or '*over* content but *as* the content of nations, nationalism and modernity' (French 1999: 251). At face value, the magazine might seem a return to the kind of print capitalism on which Anderson initially relied for his thesis; after all, as a serialized form, there is some correspondence between the magazine and the newspaper, which Anderson considers 'an "extreme form" of the book' (2006: 34). Yet magazines, like the brochures, postcards, photographs, and posters that have provided material for other germane scholarly studies in tourism studies, offer pathways into, around, and through destinations. In what follows I attend particularly to their use of advertisements and maps because of their emblematic association with tourism. I regard these visual representations, a central part of the industry's material apparatus and scopic regime, as 'vehicles through which the performative spaces of tourism are activated and place is created, enlivened, and (re) enacted' (Scarles 2009: 485).

The selected magazines are important because they tell us about the intimate but uneasy 'connective tissue' (Flaherty 2016: 104) of tourism, state, and society at two critical periods of Mexico's reconstruction as a modern nation (Revolution and 'counter-revolution') that are not always studied together. The magazines' start and end dates of publication delimit a near fifty-year interval (1925–1971) that encompasses two decisive but usually bifurcated phases of Mexico's history: the immediate post-revolutionary reconstruction (and the country's so-called 'cultural renaissance') and the less studied economic 'miracle' of the 1940s and successive decades of modernization. The latter were the mid-century PRI*ista* years of political consensus or so-called *dictablanda*, seen by some (before the economic shocks of the early 1970s) as a cultural Golden Age, which, though previously deemed either 'unfashionable' or 'irrepressible' in scholarly terms, have been garnering significant interest recently from 'historically-minded Mexicanists' (Gillingham and Smith 2014: 6).[7] This diachronic study of the two magazines thus allows for a more extensive, comparative consideration of tourism and its cultural ramifications across periods in Mexico that conventionally have been compartmentalized in the scholarship. Much of the valuable work on this subject to date ends when the tourist success begins (that is, in 1946) or else leaps to the more contemporary experience of tourism in the late twentieth century. Either way, in doing so, it offers only a truncated view of an industry whose ebb and flow beyond its initial period of success and prosperity to its expansion after WWII and instability during the Cold War and throughout the radical (geo)political changes of the 1960s also warrants scrutiny.[8]

In bringing these two magazines and periods together, my aim is not to trace a simple linear narrative about tourism's rich and variegated promotional apparatus from Revolution to counter-revolution. As Gil Joseph et al. observe, things are more complicated than even a revisionist metanarrative of post-revolutionary Mexico allows (Joseph et al. 2001: 7). Rather, what transpires in the comparison of these magazines across those decades in Mexico, in which the state's engagement with tourism altered significantly, is the striking persistence and rehearsal of similar visual tropes, themes, and contradictions. Further, this study also brings to light previously unknown forms of recycling of key actors, rhetoric, and iconography from pre-revolutionary eras within the modern period, as Mexico navigated an ambivalent path towards and within modernity. In essence, the book reveals how the magazines' textual and paratexual apparatus conjugated the perennial tension between tradition and modernity, and between culture and commerce, that was then being articulated and interrogated in Mexico on a larger literal and political canvass. For, as Tenorio Trillo writes, the modern nation is always a particular expression of 'the continuum of interactions between … tradition and modernity, non-Western and Western trends, popular and elitist expressions and interests', an understanding of which exposes 'the fragility, the artificiality, and contingency of modern nationalism' (Tenorio Trillo 1996: 242–243).

This book combines the findings of archival work on *Mexican Folkways* and *Mexico This Month*, both of which are un-digitized, with historiographical research and close reading of the magazines' aesthetic and textual features. In this regard, it contributes to an emerging branch of periodical scholarship in Mexican studies, including works on the 'ubiquitous and vulgar' popular comic books of the 1940s onwards by

Anne Rubenstein (1998) and, more recently, working class and political titles by John Lear (2017). Insofar as it mobilizes methods from and engages with existing scholarship in Mexican cultural history, periodical studies, and visual culture, this book aims to speak to scholars from those disciplines and others that have yet to coincide in the study of this hybrid and intercultural periodical form in Mexico. It provides the first 'biography' of each magazine, taking into account the wider media ecology of publication and distribution contexts as well as financial support, while also considering their design features (page length, use of illustrations, advertisements, paper and so on). Indeed, the book conducts analysis of key paratextual features—advertising and maps—that have themselves yet to be subject to broader scholarly enquiry. Such nominally 'marginal' images, this book argues, though they are commonly considered peripheral in terms of the history of periodicals, merit serious scrutiny. In doing so, the book also engages with recent developments in the study of advertising and cartography in different disciplines including cultural studies, geography, history, sociology, and tourism studies. In sum, this book moves beyond an exclusively text-based or semiotic analysis of the magazines' visual and narrative contents to embrace a historically situated interdisciplinary methodology, informed by the very constitution of its distinctive object of study, which 'does not just make history [but] … *is* history' (Bulson 2012: 268).

While each of the following chapters comprises an analytical and methodological enquiry into a distinct feature of the magazines' visual apparatus, Chapter 1 deals with contexts and frameworks in broad terms. It provides a detailed introduction to the book's historical, industrial, and cultural contexts and further situates its own efforts within and across relevant fields of study, including tourism and periodical studies and Mexican cultural history. It examines the value of tourism to nation formation in Spanish America broadly before considering the specific circumstances of the industry in Mexico after the Revolution. It also provides a vital discussion of the magazine as a form and elucidates in detail the particular methodological issues at stake in the analysis of this 'singular' but heterogeneous object of study.

Chapter 2 examines the use of tourism advertisements in *Mexican Folkways* (1925–1937), a bilingual periodical designed to endorse the study and understanding of indigenous cultural practices as a means of racial integration and modernization, which has since become a treasured source in the historiography of Mexico's post-revolutionary period. The chapter considers advertising in the context of the magazine's genesis and dissemination as well as within the context of a reconceptualization of Mexican nationalism and a burgeoning consumer culture during Mexico at that time. It contends that attention to such paratextual features illustrates some of the central paradoxes at stake in the reliance on this periodical as a historiographical source. Such tensions resonate with other ambivalences at national level in the new Republic's ostensibly counterintuitive endeavour to deploy tourism as a means of recovery and reconstruction after the Revolution. Methodologically, the chapter adds to content and textual analysis of advertisements for El Buen Tono cigarettes and Mexico City hotels, a historically situated consideration of the context of their, and the magazine's, production. In doing so, it spotlights what elsewhere Garrigan (2012) has called 'the dialectical embrace of patrimony and market' at various layers of the periodical and illuminates untold forms of recycling of processes and stakeholders that had been fundamental to nation-building during the *Porfiriato* in the re-making of modern Mexico after 1920. The chapter aims not simply to re-tell an already familiar story about Mexico during that period of national reconstruction. Rather, it argues that if one of the much-lauded innovations of *Folkways* was its attempt to present the 'real' Mexico as rural and indigenous, its commercial associations and engagement with the 'new science' of advertising also grounded it firmly in urban modernity and implicated it fully in the business of shaping consumer-citizens and tourists in and outside the new Republic.

Chapter 3 considers the role and ramifications of illustrated travel magazines in the 1950s, at the height of the so-called miracle. Focusing on the particular case of Anita Brenner's *Mexico/This Month* (1955–1971), the chapter attends to the function of what would become in the magazine's early years its trademark centre-fold maps, the Explorers' Maps Series. This chapter, taking its cue from scholars in geography and cultural studies who are interested less in 'maps as finished artifacts than … in mapping as a creative activity' (Corner 1999: 217), rather than consider them visual adjuncts or simple guides to the routes travelled elsewhere in written form, perceives maps as complex representations with their own narrative qualities and histories. The story of the Explorers' Maps series of *Mexico This Month* that unfolds in this chapter is one about maps as intertextual objects which, as Stephen P. Hanna and

Vincent J. del Casino argue in their work on the 'map space', 'are materially interconnected to other spaces and texts, both past and present, and are thus rich sites for the critical interrogation of tourism practices and spaces' (Hanna and del Casino 2003: xxvi). The chapter also considers the impact of capital on the magazine's endurance as a material object over its lifetime, and sheds further light on the anomalous ways in which *Mexico This Month* was invested in the aesthetics, geopolitics, and economics of tourism during Mexico's post-war/Cold-War years.

NOTES

1. In this article she pitches against those who Go Native the Typical Tourist who 'work[s] awfully hard, examining ruins, and cathedrals, and murals, and sombrero-ed peasants, and blanket-weavers [who] will become much bewildered and confused and irritable, because no one [can do that] without getting extremely fatigued and distressed', n.p.
2. *Your Mexican Holiday*, regarded as a pioneering English-language guide to the country, was researched and compiled on Brenner's honeymoon there. It was first published in New York by Putnam's in 1932 and was reissued in five further editions until 1947.
3. *Holiday*, launched in 1946 by the Curtis Publishing Company, was a relatively new and expensive yet influential travel magazine in the US market: as Richard Popp points out, although 'it would never achieve the iconic stature of *Life*, *Holiday* did establish itself as a media industry model during an era of remarkable change'. See Popp (2012: 31).
4. According to Berger, its operations nonetheless 'mirror[ed] the equally chaotic political climate' of the time (2006: 20).
5. Heritage tourism, a magnet especially to US tourists, as Alan Knight observes, apart from generating valuable foreign exchange, also 'performed a useful politico-diplomatic function … breaking down some of the ancient prejudices which vitiated US-Mexican relations'. Knight (2015: 316).
6. For a summary of the critique of Anderson, see Chasteen (2003).
7. Joseph et al. explain that the reluctance of scholars to study the latter half of the twentieth century is down in part to a fear of 'losing' Mexico, 'to en-counter little more than crass transnational capitalism, an all-too-familiar McWorld set down on the Zona Rosa', in part too because of the absence of (still classified) archival materials (2001: 14).
8. Recent studies on tourism in/into Mexico, in addition to Berger (2006), include Berger and Grant Wood (2010), Clancy (2001), Merrill (2009), and Méndez Sáinz and Velásquez García (2013).

REFERENCES

Anderson, Benedict. 2006. *Imagined Communities: Reflections on the Origin and Spread of Nationalism*, 2nd ed. London and New York: Verso.

Berger, Dina. 2006. *The Development of Mexico's Tourism Industry: Pyramids by Day, Martinis by Night*. New York: Palgrave Macmillan.

Berger, Dina, and Andrew Grant Wood, eds. 2010. *Holiday in Mexico: Critical Reflections on Tourism and Tourist Encounters*. Durham: Duke University Press.

Brenner, Anita. n.d., n.p, *Anita Brenner Papers* 30:8.

———. 1932. 'On Going Native in Mexico.' *Arts and Decoration*, August 1932. *Anita Brenner Papers* 31:6.

———. 1947a. Holiday MS. *Anita Brenner Papers* 29:6.

———. 1947b. Anita Brenner to Gilberto Figueroa, 21 February. *Anita Brenner Papers* 30:8.

———.1947c. Alejandro Buelna to Guillermo Hawley, 31 March, *Anita Brenner Papers* 30:8.

———.1947d. Guillermo Hawley to Alejandro Buelna, Departamento de Turismo, 10 April. *Anita Brenner Papers* 30:8.

Bulson, Eric. 2012. 'Little Magazine, World Form.' In *The Oxford Handbook of Global Modernisms*, edited by Mark Wollaeger and Matt Eatough, 268–285. Oxford: Oxford University Press.

Carrera, Magalí. 2011. *Travelling from New Spain to Mexico: Mapping Practices of 19th-Century Mexico*. Durham: Duke University Press.

Chasteen, John Charles. 2003. 'Introduction: Beyond Imagined Communities.' In *Beyond Imagined Communities: Reading and Writing the Nation in 19th-Century Latin America*, edited by Sara Castro-Klarén and John Charles Chasteen, ix–xxv. Baltimore: John Hopkins University Press.

Clancy, Michael. 2001. *Exporting Paradise: Tourism and Development in Mexico*. Amsterdam: Pergamon.

Corner, James. 1999. 'The Agency of Mapping: Speculation, Critique and Invention.' In *Mappings*, edited by Denis Cosgrove, 213–252. London: Reaktion.

Flaherty, George F. 2016. *Hotel Mexico: Dwelling on the '68 Movement*. Oakland: University of California Press.

French, William. 1999. 'Imagining and the Cultural History of Nineteenth-Century Mexico.' *Hispanic American Historical Review* 79 (2): 249–268.

García Canclini, Nestor. 1995. *Hybrid Cultures: Strategies for Entering and Leaving Modernity*. Translated by Christopher L. Chiappari and Silvia L. López. Minneapolis and London: University of Minnesota Press.

Garrigan, Shelley E. 2012. *Collecting Mexico: Museums, Monuments, and the Creation of National Identity*. Minneapolis: University of Minnesota Press.

Gillingham, Paul and Benjamin T. Smith, eds. 2014. *Dictablanda: Politics, Work, and Culture in Mexico, 1938–1968*. Durham: Duke University Press.

Hanna, Stephen P., and Vincent J. del Casino Jr., eds. 2003. *Mapping Tourism*. Minneapolis: University of Minnesota Press.

Hellier-Tinoco, Ruth. 2011. *Embodying Mexico: Tourism, Nationalism, and Performance*. Oxford: Oxford University Press.

Joseph, Gilbert M., Anne Rubenstein, and Eric Zolov, eds. 2001. *Fragments of a Golden Age: The politics of culture in Mexico Since 1940*. Durham: Duke University Press.

Knight, Alan. 2015. 'History, Heritage, and Revolution: Mexico c.1910–c.1940.' *Past and Present* Supplement 10: 299–325.

Lear, John. 2017. *Picturing the Proletariat: Artists and Labor in Revolutionary Mexico 1908–1940*. Austin: University of Texas Press.

López, Rick A. 2010. *Crafting Mexico: Intellectuals, Artisans, and the State After Revolution*. Durham: Duke University Press.

Méndez Sáinz, Eloy, and Mario Alberto Velásquez García, eds. 2013. *Turismo e imaginarios*. Hermosillo: El Colegio de Sonora, Instituto Tecnológico y de Estudios Superiores de Monterrey Campus Sonora Norte.

Merrill, Dennis. 2009. *Negotiating Paradise: U.S. Tourism and Empire in Twentieth-Century Latin America*. Chapel Hill: University of North Carolina Press.

Mirzoeff, Nicolas. 2015. *How to See the World*. London: Penguin.

Mraz, John. 2009. *Looking for Mexico: Modern Visual Culture and National Identity*. Durham: Duke University Press.

Popp, Richard. 2012. *The Holiday Makers: Magazines, Advertising, and Mass Tourism in Postwar America*. Baton Rouge: Louisiana State University Press.

Rubenstein, Anne. 1998. *Bad Language, Naked Ladies, and Other Threats to the Nation: A Political History of Comic Books in Mexico*. Durham: Duke University Press.

Scarles, Caroline. 2009. 'Becoming Tourist: Renegotiating the Visual in the Tourist Experience.' *Environment and Planning D: Society and Space* 27: 465–488.

Tenorio Trillo, Mauricio. 1996. *Mexico at the World's Fairs: Crafting a Modern Nation*. Berkeley and London: University of California Press.

Open Access This chapter is licensed under the terms of the Creative Commons Attribution 4.0 International License (http://creativecommons.org/licenses/by/4.0/), which permits use, sharing, adaptation, distribution and reproduction in any medium or format, as long as you give appropriate credit to the original author(s) and the source, provide a link to the Creative Commons license and indicate if changes were made.

The images or other third party material in this chapter are included in the chapter's Creative Commons license, unless indicated otherwise in a credit line to the material. If material is not included in the chapter's Creative Commons license and your intended use is not permitted by statutory regulation or exceeds the permitted use, you will need to obtain permission directly from the copyright holder.

CHAPTER 2

Tourism, Nation-Building, and Magazines

Abstract In two sections, this chapter examines, first, the correspondence between tourism and nation-building in conceptual and material terms and, second, the magazine as a paradigmatic expression in print culture of that concurrence. The first section, drawing on recent scholarship in tourism and Latin American studies, situates the book's focus on Mexico within the country's remarkable emergence from the Revolution during the 1920s and onwards, contextualizing that significant juncture within the history of organized tourism there since the late nineteenth century to the present day. The second section, drawing on examples from the book's corpus of magazines, elucidates the unparalleled properties of the periodical as an object of study within those contexts and considers ensuing methodological issues.

Keywords Tourism · Revolution · Nation-building · Modernity · Mexico · Magazines · Consumerism · Archive · Methodology

This chapter considers the cultural, historical, and methodological contexts that are at the heart of this book's enquiry. It provides an essential frame of reference for the chapters that follow and offers a timely intervention into current methodological debates in periodical studies. In two sections, the chapter examines, first, the correspondence between tourism and nation-building in conceptual and material terms and, second, the magazine as a paradigmatic expression in print culture of that concurrence. Drawing on recent scholarship in tourism and Latin American studies, the first section situates the book's focus on Mexico within the country's remarkable emergence from the Revolution during the 1920s, contextualizing that significant juncture within the history of organized tourism there since the late nineteenth century to the present day. It then locates this book's endeavours within the growing scholarship on tourism and nation-building in Mexican cultural history and recent considerations of the relation in Spanish America between tourism and visual culture. The second section, drawing on examples from the book's corpus of magazines, elucidates the unparalleled properties of the periodical as an object of study within those contexts. It offers comprehensive observations on the magazine as a unique form, considering its defining admixture of visual and written material and its dialectical functions as archive and store. The question of different categories of magazine (e.g. the popular vs the more high brow) and their associated symbolic capital is also addressed here with specific regard to the magazines selected for study in this book, among the aims of which are to advance our appreciation of such texts beyond their value as source materials and to enrich our understanding of the diversity and complexity of the periodical field. The rich heterogeneity of this serialized form of print culture has broader methodological implications, which are pursued in the chapter's final section.

Tourism and Nation-Building

Tourism has often been mobilized by developing countries as a form of nation-building, especially in the wake of economic and/or political crisis.[1] Indeed, as Florence Babb has shown in her ethnographic work on the subject in Latin America, 'tourism often takes up where social transformation leaves off and even benefits from the formerly off-limits status of nations that have undergone periods of conflict or rebellion' (2011: 2). At face value, however, that coincidence of tourism and revolution (as it has manifested in Latin America) might seem anomalous, the two scarcely compatible phenomena: the first, the commercial organization of 'leisure' travel and sightseeing, which are often regarded as superficial and exploitative practices; the second, the forcible overthrow of a government in the name of social justice.[2] Further scrutiny of the experiences and 'logic' of the two, however, reveals a closer affinity that is camouflaged by those definitions. Dean MacCannell hints at this association, notwithstanding the early admission in his groundbreaking book *The Tourist* that, 'Originally I had planned to study tourism and revolution, which seemed to me to name the two poles of modern consciousness – a willingness to accept, even venerate things as they are, on the one hand, a desire to transform things on the other' (1976: 3).[3] In fact, MacCannell's study insinuates an epistemological affiliation between tourism and revolution that belies that assertion. That is, while at first he articulates his understanding of the two in binary terms, MacCannell goes on to characterize them as exemplary, synchronous components of modernity: if '"The revolution" in the conventional, Marxist sense of the term', he writes, 'is an emblem of the evolution of modernity', '"the tourist" is one of the best models available for modern-man-in-general' (1976: 13, 1). Indeed, the very idea that tourists 'accept/venerate things as they are' is revealed on closer inspection to be a limited understanding of their activities. For, as MacCannell himself and other scholars of tourism have demonstrated, it is curiosity and desire for *engagement* with rather than pure *detachment* from culture and society that fuel the tourist's motivation to travel. Moreover, if we think of transformation as the core, driving impulse of both revolution and tourism, a closer correlation of the two phenomena starts to look more conceptually viable. The former is about a metamorphosis of political structures and institutions, while in the latter, the change of the traveller's environment, from home to away, may entail a form of 'internal travel ... an exploration, or discovery, of feelings' or identity (Clark and Payne 2011: 117). Each involves a transgression of boundaries, whether it be of socio-political classes, spaces, geographical frontiers, or emotions. In short, to invoke and adapt Eric Leed's seminal observations on travel, in empirical and figurative terms, both tourism and revolution '[are] a source of the "new" in history ... creat[ing] new social groups and bonds' (1992: 15).

The correlation between tourism and revolution is more than conceptual, however: it has strong historical foundations in various Spanish American nations that have undergone armed conflict identified as revolutionary. Countries such as Cuba, Nicaragua, and Mexico have at different junctures of the twentieth century become magnets for what Maureen Moynagh calls political tourism, precisely because of their histories of armed rebellion.[4] Most often the purview of mobile 'vulgar cosmopolitans' who 'pursue affiliation and belonging with struggles ostensibly not their own', for Moynagh, political tourism has an affective dimension, as it expresses a form of 'long-distance empathy' with anti-imperial and anti-fascist struggles across the world, and seeks to de-construct international borders 'in acts of affiliation and commitment' (2008: 6).[5] If the 1959 Revolution, and the imposition of the 1962 US embargo on travel and trade, discouraged the kind of mass tourism to Cuba seen in the 1950s, the island nonetheless became a hub for intellectuals, writers, artists, and activists who flocked there to see revolutionary society and contribute to processes of social transformation then taking place (Jayawardena 2003). 'Tourist-revolutionaries' from North America took circuitous routes to help cut sugar cane while others of an intellectual or artistic stripe (such as Susan Sontag, Mario Vargas Llosa, Jean-Paul Sartre, and Simone de Beauvoir) went 'to make of their observation an active participation' (Fay 2011: 408). Nicaragua, following the 1979 Sandinista victory, hosted an analogous horde of what poet Lawrence Ferlinghetti—himself a visitor to the country—wryly termed 'tourists of revolution'. Those so-called *sandalistas* included figures such as Margaret Randall, Susan Meiselas, and Salman Rushdie on similar kinds of pilgrimage to those made earlier to Cuba, though the Nicaraguan state was keen 'to shed the notion of [the country] as a place of political conflict and of danger, and [for tourists] to discover a land of beautiful landscapes and friendly people' (Babb 2004: 549). In each of these cases tourism, animated by the triumphant formation of revolutionary states, is articulated and identified largely as an exogenous, elitist, and ephemeral affair, depictions that resound with that time-honoured, yet troubling dichotomy between traveller and tourist. Criticism of tourism as shallow and superficial, which underpins that persistent but ultimately reductive dichotomy, is frequently 'more anecdotal than analytical', however (Merrill 2009: 14). Indeed, resting on a rhetoric of moral superiority, it is open to charges of superficiality of its own.[6] On this theme, MacCannell wryly observes that, 'God is dead, but man's need to appear holier than his fellows lives' (1976: 10). As he, Merrill, and others have argued, 'discounting the intellectual and cultural depth of the tourist experience' is specious as it disregards tourists' historical agency as well as their significance in international relations (Merrill 2009: 13).

These factors are crucial to the context under scrutiny in this book, although at stake here is an iteration of tourism that differs in significant ways from the kind of 'solidarity travel' just discussed—in this instance, a modern Mexico attracting visitors from far and wide for its intriguing amalgam of social reform (in land ownership, education, and popular art), pre-Columbian archaeological sites and indigenous peoples.[7] In what follows, my interest in and engagement with tourism as a category stems not only from a shared scepticism of and enthusiasm for neutralizing that pervasive travel-tourism dichotomy. Fundamentally, it arises from the unique historical context, the endogenous development of tourism as a mass industry in Mexico—rather than a niche, vertically imposed 'imperialist' affair—and to the Mexican state's attempts to foster tourism as a tool in its reconstruction after the Revolution (unlike Cuba) as 'an industry made by and for Mexicans' (Berger 2006: 2).[8] Indeed, some important work in Latin American and postcolonial studies in the last decade or so on tourism, to which this book aims to contribute, has undertaken a more considered reappraisal of its historical operations in the region. As Michael Clancy argues, such scrutiny is, if nothing else, an economic imperative: 'Tourism deserves greater empirical attention due to its sheer size in the world economy and within the developing world', he avers, since 'roughly one in every four international tourist dollars is spent [there]' (2001: 2). In consequence, much of the scholarly work on tourism in Latin America to date has tended to focus on those countries already mentioned as well as different Caribbean nations that have turned to 'tourism [as] an agent for the refashioning of cultural heritage and nationhood' after periods of particular upheaval and instability (Rosa 2001: 458).[9] Scholars in anthropology, geography, history, sociology, and cultural studies have in different ways illuminated how tourism can function 'as more than just a form of imperialism, exploitation, or profit'. In doing so, they have contributed to a shift in thinking about this industry and activity away from 'a simple system of cultural imposition' to 'an ongoing international negotiation' in which cultural linkages between the global North and South are created and produce 'ambiguous, interdependent relationships' (Merrill 2009: 1, 9). Tourism, for Dina Berger and Andrew Grant Wood, for example, and as evinced in my case studies, can operate 'as a form of potentially positive encounter … as a form of public diplomacy [even] because it is a kind of exchange among non-state actors that … can shape and even reorient perceptions of other people, cultures, and nations' (2010: 108–110). As such, in concert with Berger, Grant Wood and others, this book regards tourism as a set of complex (trans) cultural practices and encounters, for which the long-standing caricature of the tourist/tourism visualised in Duane Hanson's well-known lifelike sculpture 'Tourists', though amusing, is ultimately unhelpful.[10] Rather more useful in this context is historian Rudy Koshar's affirmation—a reminder of the association of travel in all its modalities to 'travail'—that 'tourism finds its meaning through effort, contact, and interaction, no matter how programmed or structured' (quoted in Merrill 2009: 14).

This is not to say that we should disregard the imperialist precedents and continuities of tourism: to be sure, in some circumstances tourism does resemble conquest and in Spanish America, the industry's contradictions are more than evident. The cases of Cuba and Mexico attest to this. While the industry can restore the coffers of an ailing economy (whether, as in the case of Cuba, due to the US embargo since the start of the so-called Special Period, or, in the case of Mexico in the 1920s and 1930s, as a result of the protracted armed phase of the Revolution), tourism has had adverse effects that can undermine the original nation-building aspirations at stake. In Cuba and Mexico, for example, state encouragement of foreign capitalist investment has had equally compromising implications in terms of the two nations' revolutionary credentials. In the former, the increasingly visible economic and social inequalities that emerged alongside the development of tourism in the island since the early 1990s have undermined the preservation of socialism and its egalitarian principles, a central paradox given that it is precisely 'Havana's oppositional role as anticapitalist capital [that has had] … a potent and enduring heterotopic function' in sustaining the international image of Cuba as a 'political fantasy, nostalgic commodity, and Cold War fetish' (Dopico 2002: 458). In Mexico, the pace of industrialization and the development of tourist infrastructure in the 1940s onwards (to which I return in Chapter 3), part of a 'public relations effort to convince their northern neighbor that Mexico was a safe place to invest' (Nilbo and Nilbo 2008: 42), effectively contradicted the revolutionary state's former economic nationalism as well as paradigmatic *Cardenista* land reforms. Moreover, in tandem with those inequalities arose new kinds of corruption, whether in the form of a revivified economy of sex tourism in Cuba or in diverse manifestations of political misconduct in Mexico at the start and throughout its subsequent development of tourism, as when the channelling of state resources into industrialization programmes has 'coincided with the private interests of key functionaries' such as President Miguel Alemán himself (Nilbo and Nilbo 2008: 38). Nevertheless, it is precisely the complexity of these experiences, as Babb suggests, that befits consideration of 'the ways that tourism and revolution intersect [in the region]...particularly at a time when postsocialism is heralded and globalised capitalism reigns' (2004: 553). This book aims to enhance and advance such considerations with specific regard to Mexico, where from the 1920s onwards tourism allowed the country to participate in modern capitalism and overcome the serious financial problems bequeathed by Revolution, as well as a foreign debt exacerbated by the Great Depression. For tourism in the post-revolutionary period, as Alex Saragoza writes, 'contributed substantively to the nationalization of cultural expression in Mexico and its projection outside of the country ... [and ultimately] presented the dramatic *making of the nation*' (2001: 91, 93, my emphasis). A brief contextualization of the development of tourism in the country will be useful at this juncture.

Organized tourism to Mexico from the north began in the 1880s, stimulated by an acceleration in the construction of railroads, which multiplied in number at that time.[11] Indeed, Mexican rail-road companies also became 'prolific publishers of tourist materials and travel guides' (Boardman 2001: 32), providing information on where to stay and what to do along their routes. At the turn of the twentieth century, President Porfirio Díaz invited foreigners to settle in the north of the country in an attempt to populate the region so that American immigration there almost doubled between 1900 and 1910. The following decade saw increasing numbers of Americans travelling to Mexico, a flow that would only increase with the boom in air travel in the late 1920s (famously publicized by the 'hero-tourist' Charles Lindbergh's 1927 goodwill tour to Mexico to promote commercial air transport), while the border states received a substantial boost in visitor numbers following the Volstead Act's prohibition of alcohol (Boardman 2001: 63). In addition to the 'northern bohemians ... drawn for the most part from the US middle and upper classes [who] discovered a postrevolutionary oasis for artistic experimentation, social reform, and rural tranquility', the 1920s and 1930s saw large numbers of cultural and scholarly exchanges develop between Mexico and the United States as well as an influx of travellers and exiles from Europe who sought participation in the country's 'exhilarating laboratory for revolution and modern socialism' (Merrill 2009: 3, 31). In turn, the Mexican government focused its efforts on developing tourist infrastructure in the 1930s and 1940s by constructing new and improved highways and by establishing tourism offices in all major US cities. As a result, between 1939 and 1950, tourism receipts in Mexico grew from $21.7 million to $156.1 million, the greatest percentage of which came from US visitors (Boardman 2001: 69).

During that period of rapid economic growth known as the 'Mexican miracle', Mexico's economy and society were transformed, from a largely agricultural to an urban base, through heavy investment in industrial and capitalist development. In a turn to the right initiated by Alemán, Mexico enjoyed a prolonged period of political stability (its longest since the *Porfiriato*) in the guise of a 'counter-revolution': for since 1940 the commitments to addressing inequalities in wealth distribution and foreign economic domination that had been at the heart of the Revolution had begun to looked seriously compromised. In the post-war period, Mexico also benefitted from increasingly if not entirely cordial international relations with the United States, as Mexico became 'a vital outlet for US capital and a reliable ally in the Cold War then underway' (Zolov 2010: 250).[12] Indeed, Mexico's rapid industrialisation benefitted considerably from US funds, loans, and business interests (so much so that, as Hector Aguilar Camín observes, 'by the 1960s the Mexican industrial dependence on foreign capital and technology became, as in the *Porfiriato*, quite evident' (Aguilar Camín and Meyer 1993: 162). As Mexico's ruling class became increasingly conservative, it also became more outwardly nationalistic. Investment in tourism was a significant part of this. Under Alemán, Mexican tourism was modernized, professionalized and 'made' the country modern; given 'a sleek contemporary style, [the industry] refashioned the image of Mexico away from quaint peasants, curio shops and village marketplaces toward one that was more metropolitan, up to date and business like' (Saragoza 2001: 93). As a result, during the 1950s, 'thousands of tourists and investors flocked to Mexico … to take advantage of the county's vaunted progress' (Zolov 2010: 249). Mexico also then developed a reputation as a haven for bohemian visitors from the North, who were propelled by a sedimentation across the border of 'Protestant morality and expectations of upward social mobility, on the one hand, and a rigid, racial divide, on the other' (Zolov 2010: 263).[13] In this context, longer-stay tourists became of particular interest to the Mexican government, for while the Mexican 'miracle' had been successful in augmenting their number, the type of US visitor attracted to Mexico had begun to cause concern, as Michael Clancy points out:

Border tourism, as it was defined at the time, constituted almost 60% of the total [tourism in Mexico]. Short stays contributed to relatively low spending per visit and the reputation of border areas as centres of vice and smuggling intensified. (2001: 45)

Indeed, as a consequence of social problems associated with border tourism, subsequent Presidents Adolfo López Mateos and Gustavo Díaz Ordaz 'wavered in their enthusiasm for [the industry] and were hesitant to promote it more strongly' than had, say, Alemán and Ruiz Cortínez (2001: 47).

By 1970, Mexico was drawing 2.2. million tourists, a figure that nearly tripled by 1991, thanks to growth rates over that period exceeding 5% for arrivals and over 10% for receipts. It was then in the early 1970s that newer beach resorts, such as Cancún, Ixtapa, and Los Cabos, started to become established with increasing state endorsement and investment: eventually, they would draw tourism away from the traditional centres of Mexico City, Guadalajara, and Monterrey (Clancy 2001: 62). In 1974 a significant institutional change—the elevation of the Department of Tourism to Secretaría status (a cabinet-level ministry), which gave it greater prestige and (albeit still limited) financial resources—enabled the state to intervene further in the tourism sector (Clancy 2001: 56). Mexico has since become one of the largest tourism export sectors in the Third World: 'By 1996 the country drew more than 40% of all international tourists to the Western Hemisphere outside the United States and Canada and ranked seventh in the world in popularity' (Clancy 2001: 10). Today, tourism accounts for 10% of total national employment (Berger 2006: 3). Although in recent years the spread of drug cartels and attendant violence has had adverse effects on different regions of Mexico (most notably Acapulco, the northern states but including Mexico City), tourism in the country remains a more than $12 billion-a-year-industry.[14]

Throughout its development and promotion of tourism, Mexico has had to contend with long-standing negative images of it in the US press, which stem back to the nineteenth century and beyond. These include the view that Mexico and Mexicans are 'retrograde, both culturally and racially, by virtue of their "mongrelized" mestizo image', a condition (consolidated particularly during the Revolution) apparently marked by violence and childishness, a propensity towards hedonism and barbarism, as well as an inclination for dishonesty and theft (Anderson 1998: 27).

If the country's ethnic diversity provided an account of its 'backwardness', it was also—counter-intuitively—a source of difference to be exploited in subsequent attempts to promote tourism. Advertising campaigns aimed at international travellers in the 1920s and 1930s thus tended to focus on the country's natural resources as the main attractions, later adding themes of the indigenous peoples, regional costumes, and folk arts, as well as Mexico's proximity to the United States by rail. In the 1940s, however, as indicated above, Alemán made concerted efforts to modernize Mexican tourism, to move it away from its dependency on the folkloric and to cultivate a more cosmopolitan vision of the country: 'the touristic promotion of Mexico by the 1940s signified the transition from essentialist cultural depiction to one less reliant on the appeal of authenticity, monumentalism, and folklore' (Saragoza 2001: 108). During that decade of accelerated modernization (when WWII in fact aided tourism to Mexico as it had closed off alternative destinations, especially for North Americans), in touristic representations, Mexico was sold 'as the embodiment of both modernity and antiquity' (Berger 2006: 56).[15] The result was that Mexico's reputation in the north shifted in and after WWII from that of the barbaric to the good neighbour.[16] As Berger has illustrated, the combination of the modern and ancient proved to be persuasive as well as pervasive in the visual and narrative rhetoric of tourism. While images of the *mestiza* and regional types continued to be deployed to personify the Mexican nation and its tradition of hospitality, other images used to advertise Mexico City in the 1940s onwards 'consistently compared the capital to other well known US and European cities such as New York, London or Paris' and included 'fashionable, cosmopolitan women to personify modernity in an effort to make the capital desirable and familiar to tourists' (Berger 2006: 101, 105).

If developing nations such as Mexico have deployed tourism as a panacea to economic woes, central to this endeavour have been attempts like these to counteract deleterious images in 'the international imaginative atlas' (Fay 2011: 408) in visual and narrative form. In consequence, a striking feature of recent scholarship on tourism in Latin America has been the central role played by various forms of cultural production in the methods being brought to bear on its study. Geographers, historians, and anthropologists alike have looked to myriad representational practices—including tourist posters, postcards, photographs, and travel accounts—as source material for their understanding of this industry. In her work on tourism and photography in the Anglophone Caribbean, for example, Krista Thomson observes that in order to address the time-honoured stigma associated with the West Indies as breeding grounds for potentially fatal tropical diseases (such as yellow fever, malaria, and cholera), touristic-oriented representations of the Bahamas and Jamaica depended on a domesticated version of the tropical environment and society. Nature and the 'natives' were tamed and disciplined in photographs and postcards of these sites, which were marketed as 'premodern tropical locales', conveying not only the success and entirely benign legacy of colonial rule but also encoding the kind of safety travellers could expect when they arrived in those destinations (Thomson 2006: 12).[17] In doing so, such visual images presented a 'particular Edenic (a holier than thou) image' of these nations, recreating their colonial past as 'clean, wholesome, and a world without conflict' (2006: 272). Likewise, Ana Maria Dopico notes that 'the image machine reproducing Cuba for a [contemporary] global market', while exploiting Cuba's exceptionalism, 'in fact relies on tourism's capacity to camouflage revolutionary Havana into consumable mirages, visual clichés that disguise or iconize the city's economic and political crises' (2002: 464).[18]

While existing studies on tourism in the region draw on visual forms such as photography and postcards (Thomson, Dopico) and an array of other sources including travel writing (Merrill, Schreiber), tourist brochures, and radio broadcasts (Berger, Saragoza), among other textual and visual representations, this book focuses exclusively on the magazine. It perceives and champions the magazine as an essential but hitherto overlooked part of Mexico's 'culture of the visual', whose own illustrations in the form of advertisements and maps, which are the subjects of the following chapters, to some degree evince tropes and tendencies of the kind identified by scholars such as Thomson and Dopico. While I am interested in the magazines' features, articles, and editorials, the following chapters devote considerable attention to those promotional and cartographic features of their visual paratextual apparatus, not only because of their emblematic relation to the 'industry without chimneys', but also because this kind of rich but nominally 'marginal' visual content merits scrutiny in its own right as well as in relation to the magazines' remaining content. As Hammill et al. observe, though 'periodical studies is frequently structured by an implicit hierarchy of content that privileges the story over the advertisement, the enduring over the fashionable, or, more broadly, the exceptional over the repetitive', magazines need to be understood as and for their character as miscellany, as 'interlocking systems of mediation' (Hammill et al. 2015: 6). Moreover, while advertisements and maps share the same cultural economy and contexts as other visual forms, they have yet to be fully appreciated in relation to Mexico's broader visual culture, a lack of connection that, as Magalí Carrera notices apropos of maps, is both 'curious and problematic' (2011: 4).[19] Such an oversight, to which I return in more specific detail in this chapter and Chapter 3, can be partly explained by a prevailing tendency to discount or simplify matters concerned with marketing or else to affiliate maps with a purely scientific domain, in both cases ignoring the relevance or relation of these visual forms to the aesthetic or the symbolic realms. Yet, as this book argues, such images are intimately connected to Mexico's contemporary visual and political culture. Further, when read within their historical contexts of production and in relation to the other heterogeneous material between the magazines' covers, they convey complex, sometimes even discrepant meanings. Indeed, as much as photographs and postcards, this kind of illustrated periodical material attests acutely to the ways in which tourism functions both as a commodification of Mexican culture and a complex means of cultural affirmation. Thus, by concentrating solely on the periodical form, this book does not dismiss or simplify 'the elements of *bricolage*' (Moynagh 2008: 17) that an ostensibly more variegated corpus, such as that of other studies of tourism, by Berger or Moynagh say, might appear to offer. Rather, as I elucidate in the following section, the value of the magazine as a 'single' object of study lies in part precisely in its own compositional heterogeneity (that is, that it is a visual and narrative form) and its intermedial porosity, both of which belie any reductive idea of 'uniformity' or what Mikhail Bakhtin calls 'monolingualism'. In what follows, I also argue that the magazine has an agile yet 'archival' quality that is remarkable when compared with other forms of cultural production, especially in the area of tourism, an industry with which it has a suggestive and historical affinity.

The Magazine: Store, Archive, Source

As a form, the magazine is a regular miscellany of articles and illustrations often focused on a particular subject or aimed at a particular audience/readership. It is distinguished by its contemporaneity or 'newness', that it is 'continually on the move, across time': responsive to events and developments in the area of its subject matter, it selects those that are deemed worthy of report or inclusion in its pages (Turner 2002: 183). As Eric Bulson points out, the little magazine (one of the periodical's salient forms) came of age not long before WWI and was followed swiftly by the rise of Fascism and Nazism in Europe and the decolonization of countries across Africa and the West Indies after WWII: as such, Bulson avows, '[the periodical] is not something that simply registers the shocks during these tumultuous moments; it actively responds to them by establishing literary and critical communication when it could prove difficult, if not impossible' (2017: 5). Such nimble and contingent qualities and, notwithstanding recurring predictions of its imminent demise, its continued proliferation as a form have afforded the magazine (and its 'little' iteration in particular) an innovative or experimental character that has long been put to radical ends. As Gorham Munson puts it in a charming 1937 article, the magazine has operated like a 'potting shed where very rare and usually frail plants are given a chance of blooming' (1937: 10). The currency from which such experimentation has sprung is amplified by the magazine's weekly, monthly, or quarterly appearance; the serialization or 'multiple periodical rhythms' that are also one of the periodical's defining features (Turner 2002: 188). The frequency of a magazine's publication is determined by symbolic and economic rationales that have various material and epistemological implications, for, as Turner points out, 'there is no single rhythm ... no single cycle, no single motion which somehow contains it all' (2002: 187–188). For instance, we might compare subjects that appear to 'merit' a periodical title of increased (daily, weekly) frequency, for example—current events, politics, satire—to others that have a more staggered (monthly) output, such as leisure pursuits and less topical issues. In essence, however, frequency is informed by affordability at the level of production and readership. In terms of the latter, as Richard Ohmann (1996) has shown in his pioneering work on North American 'commercial' periodicals, in the late nineteenth/early twentieth century 'mass market' magazines had to extract themselves out of the realm of luxury consumption in order to attract large audiences with money to spend: they did so by lowering their price and by selling more advertising space to cover the costs of production.[20] More fundamentally, the question of how regularly an editor can afford to publish is the defining factor: historically, many of the so-called little magazines (and others), due to financial constraints and difficulties, have either amended the frequency of their output, interrupted and/or ceased publication altogether. Such is the case of *Mexican Folkways* and *Mexico This Month*, both of which received government grants and subsidies for their publication, the precariousness of which repeatedly affected their publication schedules and, following withdrawal, ultimately sealed their demise. Such state-funding arrangements are unique to Mexico when compared with many titles in the Anglophone market that are considered in the existing scholarship on this form, though the ensuing relationship between cultural producers and the state was not necessarily straightforward: as Joseph et al. write, it was 'typically asymmetrical … [but] invariably multifaceted, and power was rarely fixed on one side or another' (2001: 7).

If the magazine is distinguished by its response to the new and by its recurrence, it also rests on a degree of belatedness. The magazine is not as urgent a publication as a daily bulletin, it does not 'meet specific, local needs in the way a newspaper does' (Ohmann 1996: 355). This, counter-intuitively, lends it a degree of 'untimeliness', although Turner suggests that the break inherent in serialization is precisely 'the space that allows us to communicate', the lapses in time in fact 'where meaning resides' (2002: 193–194). Notwithstanding, the magazine's periodic appearance means that it runs the risk of anachronism from the very moment of publication, let alone of distribution, which (when on an interrupted or unreliable schedule such as those of this book's case studies) adds an additional layer of adjournment and risk.[21] Its very *in-frequency* means that the magazine's hold on its readership might be more tenuous than that of a newspaper or a novel, although serialization (of fiction, in particular) was one mechanism for retaining (and manipulating) readers' attention and loyalty. *Mexican Folkways*, for the first two years of publication, 1925–1927, was published bimonthly and from 1928 to 1933 every three months, with an interruption in 1932. During its last four years of publication until 1937, only three issues of *Mexican Folkways* appeared, as monographic numbers on Mexican 'masters' José Guadalupe Posada and its 'own' Rivera. Its editor Frances Toor was apologetic about the discontinuous appearance of *Folkways*, due to intermittent government funding. In a 1927 issue she pledged to 'do better in the future' and promised 'an accounting' if there was any further suspension in publication; while in 1933, she lamented once again 'find[ing] myself without [the] assurance of being able to continue publication. But Mexico is a land of miracles (and perhaps there will be another for *Mexican Folkways* eventually)' (8:1, 1933, 2). On the other hand, letters from regular readers of *Mexico This Month* to lament or even sympathize with the magazine's habitual tardiness were frequently published between its covers. For example, Elaine Snobar of New York wrote on 8 April 1970 of the months of delay she waited for the magazine: 'How could we possibly take advantage of anything which happened more than a month ago?' (Brenner 1968). Meanwhile, George Blisard of Waco, Texas, was more generous about the magazine's late arrival, suggesting that 'these people who write letters complaining of not receiving issues on time … have either never been to Mexico or else spent only a little time there [for] the things that make the publishing date uncertain are the basic reasons that Mexico is such a wonderful place' (Brenner 1968). Brenner thematized this belatedness in *Mexico This Month*, acknowledging and answering her readers' complaints in the magazine's pages. On one occasion she admitted to its late publication due to their printer's attempt to bribe them for more money: 'If you have jumped to conclusions and figured it's Mexican printers who act in this way, the answer is, they don't', she wrote, 'This one was a foreigner … carried away by the fact that he's the only plant in town that does photogravure' (4: 11, 1958: 6). Brenner's broadside against time-honoured preconceptions of Mexican degeneracy here was typical of her efforts throughout the magazine to contest the country's unfavourable image in the north, a subject to which I return in Chapter 3.

In other ways, a magazine's 'infrequency' can have generative properties. Its reiterated and recurrent articulation of a particular position, rhetoric or subject matter has a legitimizing, institutionalizing function in terms of ideology and subject matter. Indeed, the lack of immediacy together with such recurrence furnishes the magazine with archival or memorializing potential, conferring a greater sense of permanence and 'authority' on it perhaps than, say, that of a newspaper. As such, even when not advertising the manifestos of a particular avant-garde movement, say (as in modernist periodicals), the magazine of any kind is a purveyor of ideology and operates as a form of manifesto itself.[22] *Mexican Folkways* is a good example of this. Insofar as 'it contributed directly to the effort to collect and disseminate knowledge about the country's vernacular traditions and cast them as part of a coherent whole' (López 2010: 103), it essentially operated as an expression or programme of state policy to integrate Mexico's indigenous peoples. Indeed, it is as a repository of this sort that this magazine has subsequently become most prized by scholars, although, as I argue in chapter 3, this in turn has lead to some significant oversights. By contrast, the enterprising Brenner actively mobilized the magazine's 'archivable' potential in discrete ways. From its inception *Mexico/This Month* was circulated to schools and college libraries in the United States (the costs of their subscriptions covered by the US government) and, during the 1960s, Brenner planned an educational toolkit, among other items, as a spin-off to the magazine. The kit was to include folk art and a film package as well as supplementary teaching material for the orientation of children of Mexican origin in the US public school system. In this way, Brenner foresaw the magazine's long-term 'social' function. As such, both she and Toor can be seen as incipient 'archive entrepreneurs' in Antoinette Burton's terms, whose periodicals contradict the tendency of 'much of the material that documents tourism …[to be] by nature ephemeral' (Boardman 2001: 17) and challenge elitist histories.[23] In broader terms, the magazine as archive in this vein complicates further the question of its 'untimeliness'. For if the magazine is ostensibly concerned with the new and the now, but, on publication and reception is always already 'belated', its archival and archivable potential (foreseen by both Toor and Brenner) is also forward-looking. For, as Jacques Derrida has famously observed, 'The archivization produces as much as it records the event' (1995: 16–17). This is a particularly significant gesture in the context of a country in the tumultuous throes of nation formation.

As a material object, the magazine's potential for individual or institutional accumulation and collection—and thus for multiple usage—counteracts the impermanence and fragility usually associated with a print medium of limited lifetime, frequency, or the kind of precarious financial arrangements on which both the magazines under examination here depended. These are the normative conditions of many a magazine's production and existence. In this respect, as well as its known/identifiable subscribers (whether private or public), we need to take account of the magazine's 'pass-along' readership, for which the sense of that belatedness/untimeliness might be even greater. To be sure, the question of readership is complicated: a magazine's specialist theme or subject matter does not necessarily mean a 'coherent' or bounded audience, with the result that reader numbers are always going to be approximate, if not perhaps ultimately unknowable. Nevertheless, it is essential to acknowledge the undetected/able ways in which magazines circulate synchronically and diachronically beyond the subscription list and outside of the archive, that is, their wider, less formal dissemination and survival in the

Fig. 2.1 Front cover of *Mexico This Month*, 3:1, 1957

fuzzier realms of cultural memory. *Mexican Folkways* and *Mexico This Month* are instructive in this respect. Though Toor had at first intended to publish exclusively in Spanish for a Mexican readership, she was persuaded by the North American anthropologist Franz Boas to publish a bilingual version of the magazine. For many years in Mexico, 'though edited by a foreigner, [the magazine] won credibility domestically' in part because of its subject matter, in large part too because most of its contributors were Mexican. *Folkways* thus had contemporary reach and influence on either side of the Mexico–US border (López 2010: 102–103; Hellier-Tinoco 2011: 63).

Mexico This Month was also well received in the north in reviews in titles such as *Sunset* and *Esquire*, where it was favourably compared with the *New Yorker* (Fig. 2.1). In a bulk 'controlled circulation' arrangement that was part of its state sponsorship from Nacional Financiera, *Mexico This Month* was also distributed to Mexican consulates and embassies across the world, which allowed it to reach readers at home, in the north, as well as in Europe and Asia. Composed by both Mexican and North American writers and artists, and providing reading material to audiences located often well beyond Mexico's borders, both titles testify to the globality of the magazine as a form, offering 'a place in which writers, readers, critics, and translators could imagine themselves belonging to a global community that consisted of, but was not cordoned off by, national boundaries' (Bulson 2012: 268). This is not to overstate the extent or depth of these magazines' networks and influence, nor to disregard their darker side: as Bulson puts it, the more a magazine travels, 'the less [can] be known about where it was ending up, how it was being read, and by whom' (2017: 16).[24] Nevertheless, it is important to acknowledge the hemispheric, intercultural authorship and readership at stake in the titles considered in this book, within the context of a unique geopolitical relationship during the period in question, which has few parallels elsewhere.[25]

If the magazine's archival impulse and archivable potential resides in questions of subject matter, frequency, and readership, there are singular and complex implications of its discontinuous form, some of which are particularly pertinent to the experience of travel and tourism. The magazine is a composite text of articles, illustrations, photographs, letters, and advertisements: an astonishing miscellany of material that, as Ohmann observes, recalls the mixed stock of '[warehouses] of the odd ... the notable [and] ... of the commonplace' (1996: 223). As such, the magazine is quite a different order of text to, say, a book, although the total number of published pages over its lifetime might be comparable to or even exceed the length of a late nineteenth-century, modernist, or postmodernist literary novel.[26] The magazine's etymological roots in the French *magasin* and the Arabic *makzin/makzan* ('storehouse') are suggestive in this respect. In the formal juxtaposition of written genres and visual material, their arrangement in sections of similar order and location in each issue, magazines of all kinds sort their material into different sections that resemble the profuse and miscellaneous stock of the department store or warehouse. The arrangement, in 'small sections ... [that] appear month after month under the same title [allows the reader] [to] regularly revisit her favourite [sections or] displays' and provides a sense of orientation and familiarity (Ohmann 1996: 225). Categorizing writing further into unnamed but familiar genres (fiction, adventure, sport and so on), the magazine appeals to and accommodates the diversity and individuality of readers' tastes (Ohmann 1996: 225). Notwithstanding, as Ohmann has observed, these anthologies of diverse genres of writing and image are all collectively engaged in 'pointing, describing, and enumerating ...[in] a rhetoric of taxonomy and accumulation' (1996: 230). The experiences of visiting a department store (principally, observation and consumption) are thus invoked in the magazines' pages in aesthetic, thematic, and phenomenological terms. If, for Ohmann, the magazine editor thus becomes 'like a tour guide, pointing to this thing as notable, that as interesting, another as ... curious' (1996: 230), Richard Popp's description of 'popular' travel magazines such as *Holiday* as 'geographic galleries' (2012: 5) also aptly captures the particular resonance of that analogy between this

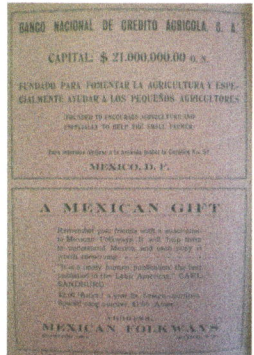

Fig. 2.2 Advertisements in *Mexican Folkways*, 4:1, 1928

print form and the experience of tourism.[27] Indeed, tourism is bound up not only in visual forms of appropriation, as John Urry and David Spurr, among others, have noted, but fundamentally also with acts of consumption, for as Hammill and Smith remind us, 'travel can be reduced to a series of expenditures: a cruise, railway journey, or road trip; accommodation; dining and drinks; sightseeing and tours; souvenirs and photographs – all have a price tag attached' (2015: 147). The Spanish term *revista* retains a strong sense of the repeated visual inspection—or 're-vision'—at stake in magazine reading, as well as in the analogous experiences of shopping and tourism. In this respect, *Mexican Folkways* and *Mexico This Month* were not only 'guides' to Mexico and archives of folklore, tradition, and culture. They functioned in literal and figurative terms as catalogues, offering a monitored, respectable space (like that of the department store) for readers to peruse and experience new forms of cultural and consumer citizenship. The magazine is a store not only in the sense that it might articulate a particular vision of Mexico for 'consumption' or advertise commodities for sale in its pages. The visual or material presentation of the magazine can announce its own potential as a commodity. As discussed further in Chapter 3, both Toor and Brenner produced special (bound) numbers of their magazines and produced pull-out sections for sale separately from the periodicals' regular issues (Fig. 2.2).

The magazine, straddling cultural and commercial arenas, is a hybrid, collective and intermedial form, its production and design the result of the collaboration of writers, artists, photographers, and readers, not to mention advertisers, publishers, 'sponsors' and distributors.

It is fundamentally dialogic on three levels, as Suzanne Churchill and Adam McKible (2007) have emphasized: it is dialogic within its own pages, in the interplay between different magazines, as well as in relation to the larger public sphere. Questions of authorship, taking named, pseudonymous and anonymous forms can, as with readership, be difficult to disentangle. (This is especially the case in a bilingual title such as *Folkways*, which printed mostly simultaneous, sometimes anonymous translations of its articles in English and Spanish.) Nevertheless, for all its discontinuity (of form and publication schedule), the magazine can gain coherence from a coterie of established contributors with a shared 'world view', or from continuous editorship.[28] In the case of *Mexican Folkways*, the two anchors were founding editor Toor and the magazine's art editor, a post that was briefly held by Jean Charlot and then Diego Rivera; there was also a core of contributing editors including Salvador Novo, Carleton Beals, and Tina Modotti. Likewise, *Mexico This Month* was only ever edited by Anita Brenner, who had contributed to the inaugural issue of Toor's periodical. Both women were inveterate travellers and travel writers, authors of well regarded and much-reprinted travel guides to Mexico. In this respect, Toor and Brenner can be thought of as *archons* in Derrida's formulation of that figure; that is, guardians 'accorded the hermeneutic right and competence ... the power to interpret the archives' (Derrida 1995: 2).[29] Driven by a personal and public archive fever, editors such as Toor and Brenner endeavoured to ensure the 'security' and continuity of their magazines' content and publication (insofar as they could in the funding and media landscapes of their eras). In a 1926 issue of *Folkways*, Toor lamented that 'if I personally didn't carry out all the labours from distributor to editor, only for the pleasure of seeing that the magazine continues publication, it wouldn't exist' (1:4, 1926, 29). Meanwhile, Brenner was known for her 'indomitable will, definiteness of purpose and unwillingness to brook criticism or suggestion' in the editorship of *Mexico This Month* (Brenner 1959). This testifies to the editor not only 'act[ing] like [a] narrator' over a magazine's lifetime but, like its contributors, also taking on the role of character (Bulson 2012: 272). Such long-term editorships speak once again to that notion of jurisdiction mentioned earlier—the magazine as 'institution'—as well as to the cross-fertilization of different transnational intellectual networks in print culture in Mexico during this period. They also speak to the prolonged, dynamic activity of women magazine editors in Mexico at that time, further consideration of which lies beyond the scope of the present study but of which there is a respectable tradition in Spanish America more widely.

In sum, the magazine is a discontinuous but coherent form: contemporary, 'spontaneous' but untimely, it has suggestive, dialectical affiliations to both store and archive. It is a malleable, mobile, and very much public work: a rich and complex assembly of material that raises the possibility, indeed, urgency of a number of potential methodological approaches to its study. In general terms, following Peter Brooker and Andrew Thacker, the magazine's composite form requires us to consider what they call the internal and external periodical codes. That is, the magazine obliges us to take into account its textual and design features (page layout, length, number, use of illustrations, ads, and type of paper and so on). Equally important, however, is its materiality, the 'media ecology', distribution contexts, and financial support, the 'business' end of operations. To date, these features have tended to be studied unsystematically or in separatist fashion, by scholars working in distinct disciplinary silos whose findings have been published either in ad hoc publications or in editions of anthologized essays about a particular country/region's print culture, rather than in sustained monographic studies or series. Examples include work in sociology on, say, the portrayal of masculinity or femininity in popular lifestyle magazines (Winship 1987) or Catherine Lutz's and Jane Collins's ethnographic study of *National Geographic*, based on semi-structured interviews, reader surveys, and analysis of the magazine's photography (1993). There is also work by historians, such as Lydia Elizalde (2007) or Saul Sosnowski (1999), whose editions of collected essays on periodical culture in Latin America provide helpful introductory overviews. In the Americas, it is notable that the fine, now canonized monographic works on single and singular periodicals—by authors such as John King (on *Sur* and *Plural*), Richard Popp (on *Holiday*), and Guillermo Sheridan (on *Los contemporáneos*)—are relatively few in number and although they are invaluable cultural histories they conduct little analysis of their magazines' textuality (their internal structure, external design, and shape).

Although, of course, 'there is no one way "to do" periodical studies' (DiCenzo 2015: 36), perhaps there is something about the relentless novelty and perceived ephemerality of magazines, to which I referred above, that has worked against either more coherent or consistent forms of engagement with them and/or the establishment of a well-defined set of methodological frameworks in the field. To be sure, the question of number and scale is significant here, as Bulson explains: 'There are too many magazines to account for, somewhere in the tens of thousands, maybe even more. ... the impossibility of collecting ... empirical data has a lot to do with the size of the print runs and the fragility of the materials' (2012: 269). Whether in terms of locating a full and complete print run of a magazine or mapping the periodical culture of a particular period or region, addressing what Scott Latham and Robert Scholes call the holes in the archive can be a difficult task. Scholarly 'search and rescue' work (Bulson 2012: 285) has been endeavouring to address these very issues, to arrest the magazine's ad hoc diffusion and to salvage it from its hitherto vulnerable existence. The burgeoning number of digital archiving projects and periodical collections in the Anglophone world (from JSTOR, Project MUSE, to the Modernist Journals Project of Brown University, among others) attests to this. The publication of anthologies and volumes such as the *Oxford Critical and Cultural History of Global Modernist Magazines* and the establishment of journals such as the *Journal of Modernist Periodical Studies*, societies and associations for the study of periodicals in different regions, such as RSVP and RSAP in the United States and ESPRiT and NAPS in the UK, are further significant developments.[30] Yet, while on one level such activities attest to the growth of a veritable academic industry, there is much still to be accomplished especially in non-Anglophone regions of the world, where circumstances in what Patrick Leary has called the 'offline penumbra' (Hammill et al. 2015: 4) remain far from the rather utopian situation described by Bulson, who avers that 'from now on it will be impossible *not* to know the little magazine through ... digital technologies, interfaces, and archives' (2017: 32).[31] In chorus with Leary, Maria DiCenzo rightly points out that one of the risks with digitization 'is that if it is not there many assume it does not exist' and, in fact, it is not a question of 'how *much*, but, rather, how *little* [periodical material] is available in digital form' (2015: 31). In this respect, though not discounting the value of digitization, and mindful of the challenges presented by international archival work with analogue periodical forms, scholars of Modern Languages or in languages other than English, especially those of us working in interdisciplinary, transnational contexts (and less wedded to the traditions of single-author study), are well placed to make advances in periodical knowledge and scholarship. As DiCenzo argues, ongoing work with print and manuscript sources is critical and 'will play a central role in keeping the offline penumbra on the radar' (2015: 32). This is one of the central endeavours of this study.

In essence, one of the essential tasks for scholars of magazines in whichever format is to adopt a catholic approach to the very categories that have emerged to date to define and delimit them. This requires engaging with the high and the middlebrow, identifying and acknowledging the overlap between them as well as their differences. It is about moving away from the 'valorizing of literary and artistic ventures over commercial enterprises' that has characterized periodical studies to date, to counteract the prevailing tendency identified by Robert Scholes to 'exclude middles and emphasize extremes' (2007: 218). While categories can be useful frames of reference, it is also necessary to acknowledge the porosity and fragility of their boundaries in practice, especially in active 'dis-identifications' with criteria—or 'brows'—that have been defined from the top down (DiCenzo 2015: 30). Indeed, as Churchill and McKible aver, 'attention to the wide array of periodicals can [only] enhance our understanding of modernity' (2007: 7).[32] I emphasize this point because it is without a doubt that it is the little magazine in English, the fruit of the institutions that sustained and promoted modernism, which has become paradigmatic in periodical studies. Though it is a term that 'cannot be applied universally' (Bulson 2012: 269), two features distinguish the so-called little magazines. First, that they have lived what Brooker and Thacker call 'a kind of private life' on the margins of conventional culture, from where they articulate adversarial positions on the 'new'. A second characteristic is their putatively non-commercial nature, that they ran on a small budget and had short print runs. As such, the little magazines spoke to a very limited group of so-called 'intelligent' readers (usually no more than one thousand), the small circulation 'seen as a marker of success in reaching [those] high in cultural capital' (Brooker and Thacker 2010: 7).[33] Recent work on modernist magazines has shown, however, that they by no means eschewed commerce entirely, either through advertising or deploying aspects of visual culture associated with it, and that some little magazines did reach larger audiences (issues to which I return in the next chapter).

The magazines of this book's corpus testify to the need to take an expansive, inclusive view of the form. In fact, the particularities of my case studies' content, composition, and circulation distinguish them in the publishing contexts of their day and from the kind of titles that have principally concerned scholars in periodical studies to date, the 'little' modernist magazine of the kind analyzed and/or anthologized in the Anglophone tradition by Brooker and Thacker and in Latin America most notably by King. *Mexican Folkways* and *Mexico This Month* cannot be considered equivalents to modernist serials, though they have some significant things in common with them (the use of manifestos, and, in the case of *Folkways*, a strong affiliation to an artistic avant-garde tradition and an unknown but probably small circulation). A significant example of cross-fertilization between such categories is the statement of objectives by the more obviously 'popular' *Mexico This Month* in the form of a manifesto, the trademark of the avant-garde periodical, which is discussed further in Chapter 3. This book enquires into magazines that were invested in mass culture (a term with heightened ideological resonance after Mexico's Revolution) which, rather than dwell on the margins, were much more obviously present in and spoke to public and national life. These titles also engaged with and in commercial activity, and, in the case of *Mexico This Month* at least, enjoyed healthy circulation numbers, though admittedly to a more modest degree than mainstream Anglophone titles such as the paradigmatic *National Geographic*. There was substantial hybridization in authorship in these magazines too. Though Brenner regarded Toor as a 'bungl[ing]' 'fool' who 'feels too superior for suggestions' (Glusker 2010: 129), like her, many other writers and artists such as Charlot and Rivera who contributed to *Folkways* and other avant-garde titles in Mexico also turned up in the pages of *Mexico This Month*. Evidently, the 'line between the mass market and the modernist magazine [was] never an absolute one' (Morrison 2001: 4), a factor that once again complicates questions of readership of these titles as well as symbolic capital across the market. These magazines' resistance to compartmentalization destabilizes categories of high and middle/lowbrow, elite and popular, as well as culture and commerce, which are the fulcrum of much of the existing scholarly work on Anglophone and Latin American periodicals. Indeed, they speak clearly to the imperative outlined by Hammill and Smith in their work on Anglophone and Francophone Canadian periodicals, that 'magazines cannot be categorized into a stable hierarchy of low, middle, and highbrow titles'. Ruling particular titles in or out of such bounded categories, say Hammill and Smith, is problematic not only because of the diversity of content which might appear in a magazine but also because of the way a magazine's character tends to alter over time, whether in response to external factors or as a result of staff changes: 'The appeal of most magazines is based on the varied selection of content they offer, and this means that they can transmit "mixed messages" in ideological terms as well as at a cultural level' (Hammill and Smith 2015: 9–10). Indeed, the material and thematic changes to *Mexico This Month* over its lifetime, which I discuss further in Chapter 3, had implications for its readers and subscribers precisely in this respect. The cancellation of its subscription to *Mexico This Month* by the San Diego Museum of Man in August 1971 speaks to this issue. Following what it saw as the magazine's 'change in nature', it wrote: 'If you have plans to make [it] a trifle more "scholarly" we might consider a[nother] subscription. But six dollars is too much for our budget to include a current events magazine' (Brenner 1971).

Another key task for periodicals researchers is to ensure that our methods correspond to the complexity of the material at hand. Notwithstanding the inextricable links between history, historiography, and periodical studies, this involves redeeming magazines from their prevailing role as source material, mined solely for discrete pieces of information or treated only for historiographical interest. To be sure, periodicals are invaluable tools for 'telling different stories about the past in a specific period or national contexts or comparatively' (DiCenzo 2015: 31), as they do in this book. Yet, the very composition, material culture and history of magazines to which I have referred behoves us to read them as autonomous objects of study which require an engagement with not only their visual *and* discursive material and the interplay between their constituent parts. We need also to take into account their narrative trajectories—the magazine's own biographies—over their lifetime in print. It is not unusual for readers or scholars to be unable 'to say much about [a] periodical as a whole' (Latham and Scholes 2006: 517). Such is the case with *Mexican Folkways*, which, as I illustrate in this chapter, is now canonized in the historiography but which has been largely 'strip-mined' for information relating to Mexico's cultural revolution alone, rather than studied as a composite aesthetic object in its own right. In this respect, in the following chapters, I take seriously the need to consider the structure, shape, and design of magazines and to pursue a longitudinal study of their entire print runs, in order to enable an appreciation of their 'narratological valence' (Bulson 2012: 272) and to counter a prevailing tendency to raid them for/of material (Latham and Scholes 2006). To take into account aesthetic, formal, and production matters within and outside their covers is part of this book's inclusive endeavour to respect magazines not just as disaggregated sources of anecdote and information, but, to draw once again on Burton's observations on archives, as 'fully-fledged historical actors as well' (Bulson 2012: 272; Burton 2005: 7).

Given the multiple transactions at stake in magazine culture (in terms of form, category, author/readership, financial arrangements, and national 'affiliations'), research in this area requires a degree of agility, expansiveness, and patience. In this regard, Churchill and McKible propose a suggestive conversational model for the study of modernist magazines that can be usefully extrapolated to the analysis of other titles including those selected for study here. Their model spotlights the 'temporal and temporary engagements, debates, and negotiations with [the field of periodicals] ...and [acknowledges] the collective effort[s] involved in the production, organization, and dissemination' of magazines, as well as 'the social, political and economic influences that shaped [them]' (2007: 14). The conversational model, for Churchill and McKible, needs above all to be inter- and multidisciplinary, that is, to apply the methods and approaches of, and involve researchers from, two or more disciplines. Such work is not only about plugging the holes in the archive of a form that historically has been (temporally) ephemeral and (financially and materially) fragile. Here patience is required, not least to access and piece together the biographies of periodicals that might not be digitized or complete in any archive, nor have any remaining business files. To be viable, claim Churchill and McKible, the discursive methodological model needs to be as diverse and co-operative as the field's very object of study (therein the need for agility), so that, as Latham and Scholes argue, 'periodical studies should be constructed as a collaborative scholarly enterprise that cannot be confined to one scholar or even a single discipline' (2006: 528). In this book, I take my cue from Churchill and McKible's conversational model in a number of respects, even if in this instance I do not adhere to the letter of its admirable multidisciplinary ambition. In essence, my enquiry, the work of a single scholar long engaged in interdisciplinary, intercultural research on the experience and practice of travel in all of its expressions, is still informed by the contextual, dialogic approach Churchill and McKible advocate to periodicals. In this instance, given their transnational and bilingual composition, circulation, and objectives, *Mexican Folkways* and *Mexico This Month* demand to be read in dialogue with coexistent periodical texts and within the context of historical developments of and between two nations (Mexico and the United States), two languages (Spanish and English), and, in light of the particularities of their author- and editorship, with each other. Such a (reformulated) conversational model is also opportune in terms of the consideration of two usually bifurcated historical periods in Mexico framed by the publication dates of *Mexican Folkways* and *Mexico This Month*, a matter to which I referred in the Introduction.

One of this book's objectives, resting as it does on a consideration of each of the magazines' entire print runs, is for the first time to tell the (hi)story, from genesis to extinction, of *Mexican Folkways* and *Mexico This Month*. This chimes with recent practice elsewhere in the field of periodical studies, as, for example, in work by Hammill and Smith on twentieth-century Canadian magazines. While mindful that no method can reproduce the experience of contemporary subscribers and readers, Hammill and Smith also underscore the necessity of reading 'simultaneously', that is, of 'comparing different items that were published at the same moment – [and] reading across different magazines' but also reading 'longitudinally across several years of the same title, in order to discern patterns or shifts in design or content' (Hammill and Smith 2015: 68, 108). In this book, such longitudinal reading is the foundation of this first scholarly study of *Mexican Folkways* and *Mexico This Month* as 'entities'. Further, although I acknowledge the value and appeal of so-called distant reading in large collaborative post-digital periodical projects, the nature of my own (necessarily predigital) research is quite different. In this respect, I share DiCenzo's broader concern with 'the option of "not reading"' provoked by the rise of computational research methods and its possible implications on reducing engagement with the very content of magazines (DiCenzo 2015: 30). There is, I contend, still much to be gained from close reading of the periodical and personal archival materials together (such as they exist), as textual analysis and discussion of the magazines' visual and narrative matter in the following chapters testify. Indeed, Hammill and Smith advocate just such a methodology that combines close reading of individual magazine issues, as well as sampling, 'accidental reading', and broad survey. My study at different junctures conducts longitudinal reading, broad survey, sampling, and close reading of the two magazines in question but in doing so makes no claim to (what might in any case be an unattainable) comprehensiveness. This is not only due to my own limitations as a 'sole practitioner' in research that is inexorably emergent, but also to the limitations of the archive itself (whose gaps in respect of the business files of *Mexican Folkways* need to be acknowledged) and the age of the periodicals in question, which means, for instance, that an ethnographic survey of either title of the kind realized by Lutz and Collins with *National Geographic* is now impossible. Fundamentally, however, as DiCenzo observes, there are also choices at stake in all of this. In this respect, this book's publication in an initiative such as Pivot is propitious as well as pertinent. Pertinent, because the radical objectives and timely publication schedule of this short-form publishing platform resound with the kind of innovation and frequency associated with the magazine as a form, as discussed earlier; yet propitious also because, once again like the very magazines I consider in the following chapters, the initiative aims to disseminate research that seeks to have a timely impact on critical and methodological debates in an emerging area of scholarship. Such is the task of the following chapters.

NOTES

1. As Peter M. Sánchez and Kathleen M. Adams point out, tourism allows developing nations 'to exploit their scenic and heritage resources potentially instilling civic pride, while simultaneously generating new revenue, principally for the achievement of more important goals' (2008: 41).
2. For a general introduction to the idea of revolution see Goldstone (2014).
3. In light of his work on revolution being unfinished, MacCannell opted to present his findings in/on tourism first, which he did to widespread acclaim, with a second edition of *The Tourist* published in 1999. I am indebted to Maureen Moynagh's observations about this connection in MacCannell's work. See Moynagh (2008).
4. In turn, political tourism needs to be distinguished from a site-specific form of trauma tourism, as defined by Laurie Beth Clark: 'the practice of visits to sites of past atrocity by those who have been directly affected and by others'. Paradigmatic sites of trauma tourism include Villa Grimaldi in Santiago, Chile, and Parque de la Memoria, Buenos Aires. See Clark and Payne (2011: 99).
5. A paradigmatic example of this from outside the region is the Spanish Civil War, which attracted large numbers of 'outsider' participants and observers in the International Brigades.
6. Moynagh concurs, writing of her reluctance to endorse the notion that 'There is some fully authentic [the thus pure] way of moving through the world' (2008: 14).
7. A more recent—and for various reasons more complex—expression of this 'solidarity' paradigm in Mexico is the Zapatista National Liberation

Army's (EZLN's) 2001 protest march from San Cristóbal to Mexico City, commonly referred to as the Zapatour.
8. Berger sums up the differences: in Mexico, there would be government-financed highways, government-regulated PEMEX companies, locally owned restaurants and tourism would celebrate and champion things Mexican, like its celebrated murals, folk art, films, and music. In contrast, Havana's tourism was not a benefit to the nation because foreigners, mostly US investors, owned many components of its tourism infrastructure including hotels, casinos, automobile dealerships, race tracks, resorts, and transportation companies. As a result, Berger notes, 'US tourists did little for the island's economy because their money fell into the pockets of foreigners, not Cubans ... Cuban tourism [could thus be equated with] a loss of national sovereignty' (2006: 19).
9. Puerto Rico offers another instructive example. For more on this see Rosa (2001).
10. 'Tourists' is part of the collection (currently in storage) of the Gallery of Modern Art, Scotland.
11. Though travel inwards to Mexico dates back to the country's origins, numbers were few since Spain prohibited foreigners from entering the country during the colonial period. See Boardman (2001).
12. Their relations were intermittently tested over issues such as the *bracero* programme (est. 1942), Mexico's stance on Cuba and later over the 1968 Tlatelolco massacre.
13. For more on such travellers, see Schreiber (2008).
14. For more on this see 'Mexico tourism feels chill of ongoing drug violence', *Wall Street Journal*, https://search-proquest-com.libproxy.ucl.ac.uk/docview/870539015?rfr_id=info%3Axri%2Fsid%3Aprimo, accessed 8 June 2011.
15. Indeed, after the war, the US military selected Acapulco and Havana as recuperation destinations for its servicemen, a choice that continued during the Korean War (Nilbo and Nilbo 2008: 36).
16. Nevertheless, as Eric Zolov points out, there was a paradox at stake in this transformation in geopolitical relations during and after the 'miracle', which was disadvantageous to both countries. On the one hand, Mexico became 'a vital outlet for U.S. capital and a reliable ally in the Cold War then underway' and as such the left-wing nationalism which once characterized the country was contained. On the other hand, as the ruling class in Mexico became more conservative, the PRI also became more outwardly nationalistic, a strategy which 'in turn generated various impediments to the full realization of U.S. goals – economic, diplomatic, and military – in the country and regionally' (Zolov 2010: 250, 259).

17. Picturesqueness, argues Thomson, was a key tool in this enterprise, erasing 'unwanted, threatening, and undesirable elements, including people, out of the social frame' (2006: 17).
18. The virtual Havana that circulates in images of the island abroad, and which 'keeps "out of sight" political conflicts that cannot be assimilated by the narratives of tourism and foreign investment' (452), rests on two main subjects: the architectural ruins of Havana, and the apparently candid beauty of Cuban faces. Both of these are objects of an erotic gaze on everyday life in Cuba and are akin, in Dopico's view, to the kind of 'international travel pornography' of *National Geographic*, which 'reminds us that in spite of all the machinery of transfer, we feel no closer to a real subject or a real experience' (2002: 477).
19. John Mraz dedicates a chapter of his book on visual culture in Mexico to a small number of illustrated magazines. See Mraz (2009).
20. The magazine's rise as a form then correlates to the beginnings and growth of mass culture, Ohmann avows, a confluence that ensured not only widespread availability of readers but also spoke to more widespread affordability, if not affluence. He argues that 'a national mass culture was first instanced in by magazines, reaching large audiences and turning a profit on revenues from advertising for brand named products … [a phenomenon that substantially] reestablished the American social order on a new basis' (1996: vii).
21. This is the case even when, in contemporary commercial or mainstream magazines, the appearance of individual issues actually anticipates the month of their publication—so that an April edition appears in March, for example—a trend that arose out of the stiff competition in the market for women's monthly magazines. A counter movement to this well established anticipatory and highly competitive publication schedule (as well as digital developments) is the emergence of a slow journalism movement with quarterlies in the Anglophone world such as *Delayed Gratification*, which rest on long-form and more considered responses to current events than the 24-hour news cycle conventionally allows. See https://www.slow-journalism.com (accessed 8 March 2018). In Latin America, analogous 'slow' initiatives might include the work of CIPER Chile (https://ciperchile.cl) and *Anfibia* magazine (http://www.revistaanfibia.com) in Argentina. My thanks to Fiona Cowood and Alia Trabucco for bringing these to my attention.
22. See Ytre-Arne (2011: 219).
23. Burton employs the term 'archive entrepreneurs' to refer to new millennium archivists such as the Lower East Side Squatters in New York. See Burton (2005: 2).

24. Indeed, he points out that while the little magazine may have been made for the world, 'it was never a medium that moved easily within it', (2017: 16).
25. The closest analogous context is perhaps that of Francophone and Anglophone Canada. For more on this see Hammill and Smith (2015).
26. As Peter Brooker and Andrew Thacker point out, just reading the contents of *The Dial* between 1920 and 1929 is about equivalent to reading twenty-one books the length of James Joyce's *Ulyssees*. Although, as they say, the level of difficulty involved is not comparable, the number of diverse contributors, 'many now lost to literary history', represent difficult challenges to the scholar versed in single-author studies (Brooker and Thacker 2010: 20).
27. In this respect, *National Geographic*'s investment in photography is paradigmatic: its photo-essays functioning 'in effect, [like] tourist trips with the editors, reporters and photographers acting as tour guides' (Lutz and Collins 1993: 32). Hammill and Smith take issue with this analogy, however, suggesting it may be 'misleading: tour groups have set itineraries and proceed altogether at the same pace, whereas periodical readers may each take a different route through a magazine' (2015: 67).
28. For more on this see Philpotts (2012).
29. During her time in Mexico, Toor edited various travel guides to the country, including a motorists' guide to Mexico, though the apogee of her ethnographic work is *A Treasury of Mexican Folkways*, an encyclopedia of traditional Mexican rituals, dances, fiestas, and ceremonies, which was first published in 1947. Toor became interested in Mexico's indigenous peoples and cultures when writing her Master's thesis at the University of California, Berkeley, where Alfred Kroeber, one of Franz Boas's former students from Columbia, taught. Once resident in Mexico, Toor worked as a researcher in ethnography and folklore at the Department of Anthropology. For her achievements as a scholar and in disseminating Mexican cultural productions abroad, Toor was awarded one of Mexico's highest honours, the Order of the Aztec Eagle. Brenner was a prolific journalist and writer, who wrote for, *inter alia*, *Atlantic Monthly*, *Fortune*, *Holiday*, *Mademoiselle*, *The Nation*, *New York Evening Post*, and *The New York Times Sunday Magazine*. She penned two well regarded and now canonized books on Mexican art and history, *Idols behind Altars* (1929) and *The Wind that Swept Mexico* (1943), for which, as well as her promotion of the work of the major figures of the so-called Mexican Renaissance, she is most well known. Brenner was also recognized for her services to tourism in Mexico by former president Miguel Alemán with the award of an Aztec Eagle, though she refused it because it was an honour designated to foreigners. As Glusker notes, however, Brenner did

accept a citation as a distinguished pioneer of tourism awarded by Alemán in 1967. Glusker (1998: 17).
30. For more on the US context see Di Cenzo (2015) and Bulson (2017). For more on ESPRiT (European Society for Periodical Research) and NAPS (Network of American Periodical Studies), see http://www.espr-it.eu and https://periodicalstudies.wordpress.com respectively.
31. Bulson warns that the increasing institutionalization of the 'little' magazine in particular could work against its trademark openness, 'unorthodoxy, opposition, and surprise' (2017: 31).
32. Matthew Philpotts laments the lack of theoretical categories for classifying periodicals, however, and proposes that periodical studies reach for new conceptual tools for more adequate ways of describing their distinctive formal properties. See Philpotts (2015).
33. As Brooker and Thacker point out, however, notwithstanding their consciously limited readerships, such magazines, in the context of the Americas especially, could nonetheless be expansive in their reach, both in the sense of their widely dispersed regional locations of production as well as in their transnational, even transatlantic, distribution and circulation.

References

Aguilar Camín, Héctor and Lorenzo Meyer. 1993. *In the Shadow of the Mexican Revolution: Contemporary Mexican History 1910–1989.* Austin: University of Texas Press.

Anderson, Mark C. 1998. 'What's to Be Done with 'em? Images of Mexican Cultural Backwardness, Racial Limitations, and Moral Decrepitude in the United States Press 1913–1915.' *Mexican Studies/Estudios Mexicanos* 14 (1): 23–70.

Babb, Florence. 2004. 'Recycled Sandalistas: From Revolution to Resorts in the New Nicaragua.' *American Anthropologist* 106 (3): 541–555.

———. 2011. *The Tourist Encounter: Fashioning Latin American Nations and Histories.* Stanford: Stanford University Press.

Berger, Dina. 2006. *The Development of Mexico's Tourism Industry: Pyramids by Day, Martinis by Night.* New York: Palgrave Macmillan.

Berger, Dina and Andrew Grant Wood, eds. 2010. *Holiday in Mexico: Critical Reflections on Tourism and Tourist Encounters.* Durham: Duke University Press.

Boardman, Andrea. 2001. *Destination Mexico, 'A Foreign Land a Step Away': US Tourism to Mexico 1880s–1950s.* Dallas: Southern Methodist University.

Brenner, Anita. 1959. Anon. to Anita Brenner, 12 June, n.p. *Anita Brenner Papers* 83:9.

———. 1968. George Blisard to *Mexico This Month*, 10 March. *Anita Brenner Papers* 107.4.

———. 1971. San Diego Museum of Man to *Mexico This Month*, 27 August. *Anita Brenner Papers* 96:5.

Brooker, Peter and Andrew Thacker, eds. 2010. *The Oxford Critical and Cultural History of Modernist Magazines*, vol. 1. Oxford: Oxford University Press.

Bulson, Eric. 2012. 'Little Magazine, World Form.' In *The Oxford Handbook of Global Modernisms*, edited by Mark Wollaeger and Matt Eatough, 268–285. Oxford: Oxford University Press.

———. 2017. *Little Magazine, World Form*. New York: Columbia University Press.

Burton, Antoinette. 2005. *Archive Stories: Facts, Fictions, and the Writing of History*. Durham: Duke University Press.

Carrera, Magalí. 2011. *Travelling from New Spain to Mexico: Mapping Practices of 19th-Century Mexico*. Durham: Duke University Press.

Churchill, Suzanne W. and Adam McKible, eds. 2007. *Little Magazines and Modernism: New Approaches*. Aldershot: Ashgate.

Clancy, Michael. 2001. *Exporting Paradise: Tourism and Development in Mexico* Amsterdam: Pergamon.

Clark, Laurie Beth and Leigh A. Payne. 2011. 'Trauma Tourism in Latin America.' In *Accounting for Violence: Marketing Memory in Latin America*, edited by Ksenija Bilbija and Leigh A. Payne, 98–125. Durham: Duke University Press.

Derrida, Jacques. 1995. *Archive Fever: A Freudian Impression*. Chicago and London: The University of Chicago Press.

DiCenzo, Maria. 2015. 'Remediating the Past: Doing "Periodical Studies" in the Digital Era.' *ESC: English Studies in Canada* 41 (1): 19–39.

Dopico, Ana Maria. 2002. 'Picturing Havana: History, Vision, and the Scramble for Cuba.' *Nepantla: Views from the South* 3 (3): 451–493.

Elizalde, Lydia, ed. 2007. *Revistas Culturales Latinoamericanas 1920–1960*. Mexico City: CONACULTA.

Fay, Stephen. 2011. 'Liminal Visitors to an Island on the Edge: Sartre and Ginsberg in Revolutionary Cuba.' *Studies in Travel Writing* 15 (4): 407–425.

Glusker, Susannah Joel. 1998. *Anita Brenner: A Mind of Her Own*. Austin: University of Texas Press.

Glusker, Susannah Joel. 2010. *Avant Garde Art and Artists in Mexico: Anita Brenner's Journals of the Roaring Twenties and Thirties*. Austin: University of Texas Press.

Hammill, Faye, Paul Hjartarson, and Hannah McGregor. 2015. 'Introducing Magazines and/as Media: The Aesthetics and Politics of Serial Form.' *ESC: English Studies in Canada* 41 (1): 1–18.

Hammill, Faye and Michelle Smith. 2015. *Magazines, Travel and Middlebrow Culture: Canadian Periodicals in English and French 1925–1960*. Liverpool: Liverpool University Press.

Hellier-Tinoco, Ruth. 2011. *Embodying Mexico: Tourism, Nationalism, and Performance*. Oxford: Oxford University Press.

Jayawardena, Chananda. 2003. 'Revolution to Revolution: Why Is Tourism Booming in Cuba?' *International Journal of Hospitality Management* 15 (1): 52–58.

Latham, Sean and Robert Scholes. 2006. 'The Rise of Periodical Studies.' *PMLA* 121 (2): 517–531.

Leed, Eric. 1992. *The Mind of the Traveller: From Gilgamesh to Global Tourism*. New York: Basic.

López, Rick A. 2010. *Crafting Mexico: Intellectuals, Artisans, and the State After Revolution*. Durham: Duke University Press.

Lutz, Catherine A. and Jane L. Collins. 1993. *Reading National Geographic*. Chicago: University of Chicago Press.

MacCannell, Dean. 1976. *The Tourist: A New Theory of the Leisure Class*. Berkeley: University of California Press.

Merrill, Dennis. 2009. *Negotiating Paradise: U.S. Tourism and Empire in Twentieth-Century Latin America*. Chapel Hill: University of North Carolina Press.

Morrison, Mark S. 2001. *The Public Face of Modernism: Little Magazines, Audiences and Reception, 1905–1920*. Madison: University of Wisconsin Press.

Moynagh, Maureen. 2008. *Political Tourism and Its Texts*. Toronto: University of Toronto Press.

Mraz, John. 2009. *Looking for Mexico: Modern Visual Culture and National Identity*. Durham: Duke University Press.

Munson, Gorham. 1937. 'How to Run a Little Magazine'. *Saturday Literary Review* 27 March: 11–17.

Nilbo, Stephen R. and Diane M. Nilbo. 2008. 'Acapulco in Dreams and Reality.' *Mexican Studies/Estudios Mexicanos* 24 (1): 31–51.

Ohmann, Richard. 1996. *Selling Culture: Magazines, Markets, and Class at the Turn of the Century*. London: Verso.

Philpotts, Matthew. 2012. 'The Role of the Periodical Editor: Literary Journals and Editorial Habitus.' *The Modern Language Review* 107 (1): 39–64.

———. 2015. 'Dimension: Fractal Forms and Periodical Texture.' *Victorian Periodicals Review* 48 (3): 403–427.

Popp, Richard. 2012. *The Holiday Makers: Magazines, Advertising, and Mass Tourism in Postwar America*. Baton Rouge: Louisiana State University Press.

Rosa, Richard. 2001. 'Business as Pleasure: Culture, Tourism, and Nation in Puerto Rico in the 1930s.' *Nepantla: Views from South* 2 (3): 449–488.

Sánchez, Peter M. and Kathleen M. Adams. 2008. 'The Janus-Faced Character of Tourism in Cuba.' *Annals of Tourism Research* 35 (1): 27–46.

Saragoza, Alex. 2001. 'The Selling of Mexico: Tourism and the State, 1929–1952.' In *Fragments of a Golden Age: The Politics of Culture in Mexico Since 1940*, edited by Gilbert Joseph, Anne Rubenstein, and Eric Zolov, 91–115. Durham: Duke University Press.

Scholes, Robert. 2007. 'Small Magazines, Large Ones, and Those In-Between.' In *Little Magazines and Modernism: New Approaches*, edited by Suzanne W. Churchill and Adam McKible, 217–225. Aldershot: Ashgate.

Schreiber, Rebecca M. 2008. *Cold War Exiles in Mexico: U.S. Dissidents and the Culture of Critical Resistance*. Minneapolis: University of Minnesota Press.

Sosnowski, Saúl, ed. 1999. *La cultura en un siglo: América Latina en sus revistas*. Buenos Aires: Alianza.

Thomson, Krista. 2006. *An Eye for the Tropics: Tourism, Photography, and Framing the Caribbean Picturesque*. Durham: Duke University Press.

Turner, Mark W. 2002. 'Periodical Time in the Nineteenth Century.' *Media History* 8 (2): 183–196.

Winship, Janet. 1987. *Inside Women's Magazines*. London: Pandora.

Ytre-Arne, Brita. 2011. 'Women's Magazines and Their Readers: The Relationship Between Textual Features and Practices of Reading.' *European Journal of Cultural Studies* 14 (2): 213–228.

Zolov, Eric. 2010. 'Between Bohemianism and a Revolutionary Rebirth: Che Guevara in Mexico.' In *Che's Travels: The Making of a Revolutionary in 1950s Latin America*, edited by Paulo Drinot, 245–282. Durham: Duke University Press.

Open Access This chapter is licensed under the terms of the Creative Commons Attribution 4.0 International License (http://creativecommons.org/licenses/by/4.0/), which permits use, sharing, adaptation, distribution and reproduction in any medium or format, as long as you give appropriate credit to the original author(s) and the source, provide a link to the Creative Commons license and indicate if changes were made.

The images or other third party material in this chapter are included in the chapter's Creative Commons license, unless indicated otherwise in a credit line to the material. If material is not included in the chapter's Creative Commons license and your intended use is not permitted by statutory regulation or exceeds the permitted use, you will need to obtain permission directly from the copyright holder.

CHAPTER 3

Tourism Advertisements in *Mexican Folkways* (1925–1937)

Abstract This chapter examines the use of advertisements in *Mexican Folkways*, a renowned magazine of folklore, visual art, and culture. It contends that attention to such features illustrates a central paradox at stake in the reliance on this periodical as a historiographical source. Methodologically, the chapter combines content and textual analysis of advertisements for El Buen Tono cigarettes and Mexico City hotels with a historically situated consideration of the context of their, and the magazine's, production. In doing so, it spotlights what elsewhere Shelley Garrigan (2012) calls 'the dialectical embrace of patrimony and market' at various layers of the periodical and illuminates untold forms of recycling of processes and stakeholders that had been fundamental to nation-building during the *Porfiriato* in the remaking of modern Mexico after 1920.

Keywords Advertisements · Cigarettes · Hotels · Photography · Style · Exoticism

Advertising has a historical association with tourism and periodicals: in the first, it has played a formative role in popularizing destinations, while in the second, its potential to subsidize the costs of publication has long been recognized.[1] Notwithstanding their ubiquity and multiplicity in the promotional apparatus of tourism, advertisements have received little scholarly attention in those arenas to date for a number of reasons. The oversight is due in part to a historical privileging of the status of the written over the visual text; in part, as David Hummon suggests, because 'of a continuing ... cultural bias against taking matters of leisure [tourism] seriously' (1988: 180); and in part also due to a lack of established or shared methodologies in interpreting such material within and across the still emerging and expanding fields of tourism and periodical studies. Although images are often described and criticized by scholars (the most common forms studied being photographs, postcards, and posters), William Feighey's complaint that 'there are many forms of visual evidence available to researchers that are not [yet] apparent in the tourism studies literature' (2003: 76) remains valid within and beyond that discipline. Advertising has been embedded in the pages of magazines of many kinds (and the press more widely) since the late nineteenth century, if not before. It has taken myriad forms, whether in advertising features/spaces proper; so-called 'advocacy' or 'institutional' advertising (in which the distinction between information and persuasion is ill-defined); or else, 'in the adoption of [promotional and/or aesthetic] strategies drawn from the practices of commercial publicity to promote the periodical' or in a 'rhythmic interchange between visual images used for articles and ... advertisements' (Thacker 2010: 8, 14). Yet the taint of leisure, commerce, and familiarity has meant that 'advertisements are narratives that are [still] rarely held up for scrutiny' (Rogal 2012: 55) in periodical studies more widely and even less frequently understood as complex, diverse, and indeterminate texts in their composition, dissemination, and reception. Recent work in modernist studies, however, which has started to shed light on the imbrication of modernism and commerce (and its attendant dilemmas) precisely through a focus on advertising in little magazines, offers a useful template for work on this subject in different forms of print media.[2]

This chapter seeks to add to the scholarship addressing that deficiency through a consideration of tourism advertising in *Mexican Folkways* (1925–1937), a renowned bilingual periodical designed to describe Mexico's folklore and indigenous heritage, which has since become a treasured, if only partially read, source in the historiography of the country's post-revolutionary period. Drawing on recent scholarship in tourism and periodical studies as well as Mexican cultural history, the chapter's first two sections combine formal and thematic discussion of the magazine's advertisements for El Buen Tono cigarettes and Mexico City hotels with findings from archival research that provide a fuller appreciation of both the genesis and diffusion of the title and the historical context in which they appeared. An exclusively text-based or semiotic analysis of such advertisements, while useful and part of the present study, has limitations that can be forestalled by this kind of multi-method strategy, which addresses the complex political, socio-economic, and aesthetic transactions at stake in these visual and narrative representations, which have been 'long regarded as ephemeral and seldom archived' (McFall 2004: 154).[3] Indeed, as Liz McFall points out, only such a historically situated focus on the context of advertising production (which 'has actually been much neglected' by scholars) can provide evidence for considerations of advertising's broader operations and influence as 'a constituent material practice in which the "cultural" and the "economic" are inextricably entangled' (McFall 2004: 5, 7). The advertisements under consideration here offer examples of some of the more frequent and conspicuous advertisers in *Mexican Folkways*. Analysis of these, which have been selected from a comprehensive survey of the magazine's issues, enables a synchronic and diachronic perspective on the aesthetic practices and politics of advertising in modern Mexico. More specifically for the purposes of this book, insofar as they promote two kinds of consumer goods closely affiliated with the industry, the selected advertisements also have a direct correlation to tourism. As such, they speak to the fundamental affiliation between consumption and the geographical imagination, which in this instance is underpinned by an investment into these goods' (far from simple) symbolic meanings as 'exotic'. In this respect, the chapter responds to Robert Scholes and Clifford Wulfman's proposal that we 'learn to read advertising [in the magazine], to decode the images as well as the texts for both ideological and aesthetic purposes' (2010: 140).

Attention to such paratextual features, this chapter contends, illuminates some of the central paradoxes at stake in the character of and reliance on *Mexican Folkways* as source material, tensions that resonate with others regarding the new Republic's ostensibly counterintuitive endeavour to deploy tourism as a means of recovery and reconstruction after the Revolution. That is, an examination of tourism advertisements in *Folkways* illuminates in the periodical form what elsewhere Shelley Garrigan has called 'the dialectical embrace of patrimony and market' (2012: 4) and sheds light on untold stories of recycling of processes and stakeholders that had been fundamental to nation-building during the *Porfiriato* in the making of modern Mexico after 1920. The chapter aims to move beyond a reiteration of an already familiar story about Mexico during that more recent period of nation-building: that is, as Thomas Benjamin sums up, that 'the cultural revolution, like everything else in Mexico during the 1920s and 1930s, was full of contradictions' (Beezley and Meyer 2010: 449).[4] This chapter does indeed illuminate a range of such incongruities. In addition, however, it perceives advertising as part of the country's wider visual culture—as much as the work of Diego Rivera, José Clemente Orozco, and other artists that *Mexican Folkways* advocated and reproduced in print—insofar as it speaks of similar issues and concerns being articulated on a larger creative and political canvass. A consideration of the magazine's advertisements reveals a series of fascinating, sometimes seemingly incongruous encounters between tradition and modernity, art and commerce. It also has important historiographical and methodological implications that are addressed in the chapter's final section through a consideration of the advertisers' aesthetic and commercial histories.

I

Mexican Folkways was the first publication of its kind in Mexico, both in terms of subject matter and languages, as it was published simultaneously in English and Spanish. Pioneering in its day, it has since become one of the most cited and revered sources among scholars dealing with Mexican popular culture, folk art, or indigenous history. Frances Toor, a North American anthropologist who had arrived in Mexico City three years earlier to study at one of the National University's summer schools, founded the magazine in 1925: in its inaugural issue she characterized herself as a trailblazing frontierswoman, who had gone among the Indians of Mexico 'under circumstances that even my cultured Mexican friends consider dangerous' (1:1, 1925, 3). The summer schools Toor attended, created by Pedro Henríquez Ureña (from the Dominican Republic), were, as López points out, 'more than a place for US Spanish teachers to brush up on their language skills or for Mexican students to learn pedagogical method'. They became 'a gathering place for intellectuals to learn about and debate postrevolutionary cultural transformation' (López 2010: 102). The bilingual *Mexican Folkways* emerged from those intellectual and cultural currents and shared aspirations to change perceptions about Mexico among foreigners and Mexicans. Thus, *Folkways* was one of many (uneasy) 'collaborations' between cultural creators and a fragile, nascent state, part of a wave of initiatives, projects, and works by writers, poets, and painters who 'treated the reconstruction of Mexico as their joint responsibility, not just the task of government' while in turn the state used anthropology, art, and narrative 'to facilitate its own insertion in Mexico's still tumultuous countryside' (Legrás 2017: 9, 11).[5] Mexican writers and statesmen, including Moisés Saenz, José Manuel Puig Casauranc, and Salvador Novo, regularly contributed articles to *Folkways* on subjects such as 'Las escuelas rurales y el progreso del indio' [Rural schools and the progress of the Indian] and the *misiones culturales*, in order to articulate the essence and purpose of Revolutionary policy.[6] In 'Nuestras escuelas rurales' [Our rural schools] (3:1, 1927), for example, Saenz, attentive to the affective character of the endeavour to 'bring that community of ideas and emotions that means Mexico' (3:1, 1927, 50, *sic*), details the goal of rural schools in respect of 'our Indian [who] has many defects, but an equal number of virtues':

> To integrate Mexico. To incorporate into the Mexican family the millions of Indians: to make them think and feel in Spanish. To incorporate them into that type of civilization that constitutes Mexican nationalism. (3:1, 1927, 50)

In the magazine's conception and execution, Toor was also influenced by the new methods and work of Manuel Gamio, who had led the excavation of Teotihuacán, and the anthropologist Franz Boas, under whom Gamio studied for his PhD at Columbia University, in a decade that inaugurated a strong and lasting tradition of cooperation between scientific researchers and institutions of the United States and Mexico.[7] Their work proposed studying indigenous traditions and local productions 'con el fin de alentar la integración racial y la afiliación a un programa modernizador que buscaba la asimilación de los elementos "artísticos" a un nuevo sistema cultural' [with the aim of encouraging racial integration and affiliation to a modernizing programme that sought the assimilation of 'artistic' elements into a new cultural system] (Albiñana 2010: 254). Boas repudiated prevailing Darwinist thinking about 'racial type' and hierarchy, for example, and proposed that races were mixed and unstable, the difference between binaries of barbarism and civilisation minimal: he urged Gamio to use his government post as inspector general of archaeological monuments to enable the study of Mexican folklore. Toor invoked both men as mentors and guides in the magazine's first issue, recounting that '[Gamio] says that this is the first publication which will present the masses of the Mexicans to the American people' (*Folkways*, 1:1, 1925, 1). Further, although she had intended originally to publish exclusively in Spanish, it was on the advice of Boas that Toor decided also to publish in English. President Plutarco Elías Calles subsequently praised the periodical for 'making known to our own people and to foreigners the real spirit of our aboriginal races and the expressive feeling of our people in general, rich in beautiful traditions' (López 2010: 104).

The magazine's subtitle—Legends, Festivals, Art, Archaeology— synthesizes much of its content, which covered Mexican modalities of expression including the *calavera*, the *corrido* and the *jarabe*, but emphasized variations in tradition, language, and culture across the country. Articles ranged from 'Costumbres mazatecas/Some Mazatecan customs', 'Marriage in a Maya Village', 'Modern Serpent Beliefs in Mexico', to others on 'The National Orchestra of Mexico', and on the paintings and drawings of Mexican primary school children.[8] For example, in vol. 5, no. 1 (1929), the magazine published a popular *corrido* about the quashing by government forces of the Escobar rebellion in Chihuahua, while an earlier, anniversary issue (2:2, 1926) reproduced a series of turn-of-the-century lithographs, portraying lurid tales and newsworthy events, such as murders by women, scandals in the clergy, and the advent of the electrical tram. Other features in the magazine singled out particular aspects of the national character or local symbolism. Anita Brenner, for example, in the magazine's inaugural issue, perceived the *petate* as a 'spiritual tradition', whose 'intimate relation to the eternal verities ... is a perfect basis for a national philosophy' (1:1, 1925, 15); while Manuel Hernández Galván depicted the *ranchero* as 'a born artist for ... song' (1:1, 1925, 8). As Luis Anaya Merchant avers, separating out its 'descriptive realism' from a Porfirian aesthetic and imaginary, *Folkways* 'era como tener una suerte de laboratorio de acceso al pasado' [was like having a kind of laboratory to access to the past] (Elizalde 2007: 131). The same is true of the magazine's sustained emphasis on music, whether in transcribing the lyrics of *corridos* or printing the musical scores of the same popular and other song forms from across the Republic's repertoire. *Folkways* thus speaks eloquently to Carolyn Kitch's assertion that magazines are 'the most dialogic of all journalistic media' (2005: 9). It is not only that *Folkways* was engaged in the exposition and dissemination of Mexican folklore to an international readership through articles such as those already mentioned, as well as through other visual and discursive mechanisms, including its responses to readers' letters, enquiries, and suggestions. In making material available from Mexico's national folk repository to a *mestizo*, metropolitan audience, the magazine facilitated intercultural encounters between attributed and unattributed contributors and readers from across class and ethnic divisions within Mexico's own frontiers as well as from either side of the Mexico–US border. As such, it consistently encouraged interaction between readers, content, and 'tradition' through processes of collective participation and creative performance. In a thematic and formal sense, *Folkways* was a dialogic, dynamic archive of Mexico's artistic and creative expressions.

As such, it is of no surprise that, in addition to Toor as general editor, artists Jean Charlot and Diego Rivera acted as art editors (Rivera designed most of the magazine's covers) and, thanks to Gamio, the magazine received a subsidy from the Secretaría de Educación Pública (SEP), the Ministry of Education that had been created by that 'great social engineer of the Revolution' (Beezley and Meyer 2010: 450), José Vasconcelos (Fig. 3.1).

The magazine's ethos and its status as a transnational cooperative proved to be its strengths but also 'its points of vulnerability' (López 2010: 104), however, as its funding was subject to the vicissitudes of Mexico's volatile political culture. The periodical's subsidy was withdrawn after Gamio's departure from the SEP following his attempts to expose the corruption of his supervisor, José Manuel Puig Casauranc.

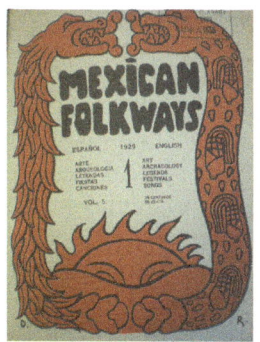

Fig. 3.1 Front cover of *Mexican Folkways*, 5:1, 1929

Puig Casauranc, with Saenz (who was appointed to fill Gamio's vacancy) later reinstated the grant, on the appeal of the poet José Frías, and eventually covered the entire costs of the magazine's production (López 2010: 104). The magazine's schedule and size speaks to those changes in fortune. *Folkways* originally appeared in 7 × 9.5-inch format, with some fifty or more pages of content. From the third issue onwards, however, it had grown not only in reputation but also in dimensions, to 9 × 11 inches, and in page numbers to an average of seventy, a larger and longer format enabled, no doubt, by the commercial advertising it also took from that point onwards, which appeared on its inside front and back pages and covers. The magazine also operated on a reduced publication schedule. For the first two years of publication, 1925–1927, *Mexican Folkways* was published bimonthly and from 1928 to 1933 every three months, with a suspension in 1932. Things changed drastically in 1931, when the Departamento de Monumentos Artísticos Arqueológicos e Históricos (DMAAH) took charge of all state-funded cultural institutions. As part of its mission to challenge foreigners' domination of social and cultural research in Mexico, it cut off all support to Toor's magazine, claiming that it was a foreign enterprise. Toor failed to secure funding for it north of the border, where the title was regarded as a Mexican, rather than a US project. In consequence, during its last four years of publication until 1937, only three issues of *Mexican Folkways* appeared, as monographic numbers on the Yaquí Indians, and artists José Guadalupe Posada and its 'own' Rivera.

In content and form *Mexican Folkways* was thus entirely *au courant* with broader state efforts to Mexicanize the nation and develop a new respect and pride in Mexican ways, during a period in which Mexicans and foreigners 'worked hand in hand to advance the ethnicization of Mexico's postrevolutionary national identity' (López 2010: 105). Such transnational collaboration stemmed in part from the fact that many Mexican intellectuals themselves had only recently returned from extended visits abroad and 'felt like strangers in their own land as they discovered the wonders of its popular classes and landscapes'; in part, also, because of a large influx of resident foreigners at that time from the USA, Spain, Central America, the Dominican Republic or Central Europe who 'aspired to speak with authority about the "real" Mexico' (López 2010: 105, 121).[9] As López has shown in his fine study of artisans and the state in post-revolutionary Mexico, what arose was a symbiotic relation between Mexican cultural elites and foreigners in the formation of a canon of authentic *mexicanidad* during the 1920s and 1930s. Toor repeatedly underscored her magazine's 'important role in the formation of the new Mexican attitude toward the Indian by making known his customs and art' (7:4, 1932, 205). Although the economic benefits of the Revolution had then yet to be felt, Toor, prompted by the editors of the *Southwest Review* to review the magazine's pioneering motivations and achievements, asserted in a valedictory feature that,

> the new governing classes have discovered the value of the Indian just as the Industrial Revolution has discovered the value of the man on the street. They have realized that if Mexico is to progress, the masses of Indians, forming two-thirds of the population, must be taken into account. (7:4, 1932, 206)

Moreover, recalling the conditions of the magazine's genesis, she spotlighted the importance of its bilingual format:

> I did not take existing folklore magazines for models. As I wanted *Mexican Folkways* to express the Mexico that interested me so keenly, it has not only described customs, but has touched upon art, music, archaeology, and the Indian himself as part of the new social trends, thus presenting him as a complete human being. And in order that the magazine might mean something to the Mexicans as well as to outsiders, everything has been published in both English and Spanish... Because of my own joy in the discovery of an art and civilization different from any I had previously known, I thought it would interest others as well. (7:4, 1932, 208)

Notwithstanding the tribulations involved in its launch and editing (her complaint that 'I have been willing to do many hard and disagreeable things' is expressive of the travails of many little magazine editors of the period [7:4, 1932, 210]), Toor avowed that the magazine's six completed volumes were 'a fair document on customs and art' and underscored the recognition it won from well-regarded scientists and subscriptions from 'the best libraries in the United States and [...] [is] esteemed even by those of the young Mexican writers who were not at all interested in the Indian' (7:4, 1932, 209). The magazine's archival and pedagogical objectives for students of Spanish as well as for readers with a general interest in folklore anticipated at its very beginnings had thus been accomplished in Toor's eyes. Further, notwithstanding its own lack of precursors and averring that 'there is [yet] nothing so complete'

(7:4, 1932, 210), Toor went on to advocate *Folkways* as a 'human and scientific' model for a pan-American magazine on the same subject matter, which 'would be of great value socially and artistically' (7:4, 1932, 211).

Alongside its spearheading of Mexican folklore, *Folkways* also placed strong emphasis in its content on contemporary visual culture. Throughout its lifetime, the magazine was a veritable compendium of images by numerous photographers such as Tina Modotti, Edward Weston, and Toor herself. There were too, in addition to reproductions of the photographs of Modotti and Weston, features on individual Mexican artists, centrefolds, and distinctive collectable front covers by Rivera. In this respect, *Folkways* could well be regarded, like many of its 'little' Anglophone counterparts, as an 'advertising house for individual modernists, as well as modernism itself' (Thacker 2010: 8), a promotional objective that fundamentally belies the time-honoured distinction between art and commerce in myriad ways, as discussed further in later sections of this chapter. Indeed, the magazine was the first outlet for the publication of Modotti's essay 'On photography'. In that piece, illustrated by a reproduction of her 1929 photograph 'Woman of Tehuantepec', Modotti disavows the category of art for photography, insisting that her main aim is 'to produce honest photographs, without distortions or manipulations' (5:4, 1929, 196). As Rubén Gallo points out, one of the reasons photographers insisted on their medium's superiority over painting and 'on its political significance during times of social revolution was [precisely its] capacity to produce an accurate reproduction of reality' (Gallo 2005: 13). In her essay, Modotti dismisses debates about whether photography is or is not art: the only important distinction, she says, is between good and bad photography, whereby the former takes into account the technology's limitations as a medium while maximizing its potential as a modern tool *par excellence*, or, as she puts it, 'the most eloquent, the most direct means for fixing, for registering the present epoch' (5:4, 1929, 196). Modotti's essay is a testament to a broader contemporary investment in Mexico in the power of technological developments—especially photography—to provide a radically new perception of reality; in essence, to revolutionize ways of seeing. Its publication in a periodical devoted to a new way of seeing the rural, the 'real' Mexico, is apposite.

Mexican Folkways, in its exaltation of the place and popular traditions of Mexico's Indians in the new Republic, documented the two major currents of reform, or as Benjamin puts it, the 'two revolutions within the Revolution' that began to arise in Mexico in the 1920s: the cultural revolution, the effort to create the new Mexican man and woman, and the social and economic one, to create 'a nation of prosperous peasants and workers' (Benjamin 2010: 449). Yet, in its sustained emphasis on the new, cosmopolitan visuality, the magazine also upheld what Gallo calls 'the other Mexican Revolution ... triggered by new media' in the years after armed conflict, whose revolutionaries were artists and writers, fighting not with weapons 'but with cameras, typewriters, radios, and other mechanical instruments ... their goal ... not to topple a dictator but to dethrone the 19th-century [anti-technological, *modernismo*-influenced] aesthetic ideals that continued to dominate art and literature in the early years of the new century' (Gallo 2005: 1). The new visual technologies, photography especially, and the mass media, of which 'print ha[d] the deepest roots in Mexico's past' (Rubenstein 2010: 600), together promised a direct and authentic record of the realities of Mexico after the Revolution, a befitting method both of documenting popular traditions and of providing a means for people to understand their new circumstances. While scholars have long invoked and acknowledged the significance of the magazine's subject matter, the following section considers a further, hitherto unstudied, aspect of its innovations: the regular inclusion of advertising.

II

The culture of consumption in which *Mexican Folkways* and other magazines of the period were invested was not a new phenomenon; Mexico itself had long earned a reputation as a 'promising and wealthy region [offering] opportunities for upward mobility [and acquisition] since the colonial period' (Moreno 2003: 3). Nevertheless, the use of consumption and material prosperity as synonyms for democracy and national identity had more recent precedents in the *Porfiriato* (1876–1911), during which period consumerism, largely an urban phenomenon associated with economic growth, 'came increasingly to define the culture and self-image of Mexicans' (Bunker 1977: 228). Stability under Porfirio Díaz had induced substantial foreign and domestic investment in the country's rail infrastructure and stimulated exports (of silver, copper, rubber and coffee) to increase Mexico's foreign trade tenfold between the mid-1870s and 1910, wealth that meant increased jobs, profits for business, and shopping.[10] As Steven Bunker elucidates: 'Consumerism can be placed within a larger Porfirian modernization belief system Alan Knight has called a developmentalist ideology, whose adherents embraced the values of moral reform, civic pride, hygiene, nationalism, and economic progress patterned after Western European and other North American economic and cultural models' (1977: 228). Nevertheless, while much of the business in Mexico then was conducted in the capital, it was not by citizens of Mexico, as Michael Johns observes:

> Americans ran most of the fifteen thousand miles of rail that carried exports to Gulf ports and US border towns and hauled foreign merchandise back to Mexico City ... streets were paved, sewers were laid, and lights were installed by American, Canadian, German, and English firms. And Spanish, German, English, and French businessmen owned the city's department stores, most of its grocery, clothing and hardware businesses and its slaughterhouse and meatpacking plant. (Johns 1997: 17)

Notwithstanding, commercial advertising gained legitimacy among the Porfirian elites as the consumption of brand name products became associated with specific ideas and where 'definitions of social norms and the ideal image of a modern Mexico centered around the act of consumption' (Moreno 2003: 86). Within this context, as large companies introduced brand names and new products in large half- or full-page notices in print, advertising, which had previously relied on simple text, modest size, and spacing (and tended to be 'relatively dry and informative', Rubenstein 2010: 602), started to incorporate new, sophisticated techniques and to use modern technologies such as photography as well as drawing. It was not until the 1920s and 1930s, however, that advertising began to be promoted more aggressively as an effective business practice among Mexican storeowners and provincial merchants, who had previously regarded it as improvident. In the post-revolutionary decades, modern industrial and commercial development once again began to be seen as the principal engines for economic growth; although this time an urban lifestyle and the consumption of advertised products became associated with 'a new form of democracy, a "consumer democracy"' (Moreno 2003: 2–3). As such, after 1930 there was a rapid expansion of 'the number of commercial graphics, an expanding range of goods being advertised, and a shift in the rhetoric being used by advertisers'

(Rubenstein 2010: 602). Indeed, from the mid 1930s onwards, government officials at the National Secretariat of the Economy (SEN) coordinated various efforts to publicize the effectiveness of advertising in increasing sales and to legitimize its practice: these included establishing a national Day of Publicity (April 23) and broadcasting radio announcements to inform the public that advertising benefited the nation by encouraging consumption. At this time, Julio Moreno avows, 'Advertising became synonymous with service to the nation' (Moreno 2003: 25–26).

Mexican Folkways regularly ran commercial advertising from its third issue onwards, on its inside front and back covers and first and last inner pages, all of them high-status spots for advertisements. The magazine's original advertisers—many of which subsequently became stalwarts in its pages—were the San Angel Inn, La Foto and the American Tobacco and News Store. Their advertisements consisted of half- and quarter-page notices while smaller retail outlets such as restaurants and others like the National University of Mexico Summer School took out 'classifieds'. Many businesses, such as Agencia Misrachi (a Mexico City store selling foreign magazines and newspapers), the department store Sanborns, the Hotel Genève and Weston's Mexican Art Shop ('leading curio and souvenir house of the republic'), offered services of specific interest to a touristic audience. At a time when 'National songs and dances [had] bec[o]me fashionable overnight, and every home had examples of the popular crafts, a gourd from Olinalá or a pot from Oaxaca' (Delpar 1992: 12), these adverts form part of an explicit endeavour underway in those decades to market the 'quintessentially' Mexican abroad, particularly in the United States where the Mayan revival style was in vogue in architecture across California, for example, and Adolfo Best Maugard's theories on creative design became available in English translation.[11] 'Cultural' and national advertisers readily associable with a 'little magazine' of this kind such as (foreign language) bookshops, art galleries, Talavera de Puebla pottery, the National Lottery, and, fittingly, though perhaps uniquely, the Banco Nacional de Crédito Agrícola [National Agricultural Credit Bank], also featured in the pages of *Mexican Folkways*.[12]

On the other hand, advertisements for construction and engineering firms, utilities and consumer goods belong to a discrete category of adverts speaking to a broader codification of modern managerial efficiency, apparently at odds with the advertisement of 'national' goods already mentioned.[13] Consonant with the way in which visual culture involves 'the things that we see, the mental model we all have of how to see, and what we can do as a result' (Mirzoeff 2015: 11), these and other advertisements do more than promote individual products—they speak to shared aspirations at consumer and national levels. Thus, advertisements for Frank McLaughlin and Co., Compañía Mexicana de Luz y Fuerza, Chapultepec Heights, Kodak and Frigidaire are about 'the consumption of advertised products, an urban lifestyle, and the modern industrial setting' (Moreno 2003: 2–3) all of which, as Moreno has pointed out in his study of business culture in Mexico, were associated with national progress and material prosperity in Mexico's postrevolutionary reconstruction. At a time when advertising '[was] a key feature of urban modernism', electricity, radio, photography, and property investment—all regularly advertised in *Folkways*—signified not only 'keys to sustain the vitality of a busy, energetic people' but also 'idioms for the celebration of energetic ambition' (Lears 1994: 180). For example, Kodak presents itself in *Folkways*, underneath an advertisement for the Mexico City photographic shop La Foto, as 'do[ing] better work', its spatial positioning and rhetoric redolent of the long-standing colonial asymmetry in north–south relations. Meanwhile, in a similar vein, an advertisement for Frank McLaughlin's construction company lists myriad services on offer ('designs – estimates – reports – appraisals') for the budding North American settler. That the opportunity for partaking in and of such activities, utilities, and services is publicized repeatedly in the magazine signals to its readers that the new Republic is 'open for business' and that, in addition to its distinctive art, folklore, and legends, the country shares or can enable similar determinations as those of its northern neighbor in terms of efficiency, modernity, and material progress.

One of the regular advertisers in *Mexican Folkways* was El Buen Tono, one of Mexico's oldest and most established cigarette manufacturers. Cigarettes are both a national good, intimately connected with Mexico's indigenous and colonial past, and a commodity with innate touristic value, which, like alcohol, have been marketed historically as luxurious souvenirs.[14] Not only do they constitute a central way in which tourists can sample local/foreign goods and culture, however. Insofar as they 'promise the metamorphosis or transformation of mood, lifestyle, and/or self-identity' (White et al. 2012: 527), cigarettes are coextensive with the very objectives and experience of modern tourism, as 'an expression of freedom and … escape from necessity and purpose' (Leed 1992: 7).

Indeed, El Buen Tono promoted its cigarettes in *Folkways* precisely as a 'therapeutic vehicle' for readers' temporary escape from the tempo of the early decades of twentieth-century life and as a paradigmatic experience of chic. In a half-page advertisement in a 1927 issue El Buen Tono's *Elegantes* brand of French cigarette is depicted as unequivocally stylish (Fig. 3.2).

The advertisement comprises elongated lettering announcing the brand while the caption ('No se discuten' [They're indisputable]) is superimposed on the image of a cigarette packet, the product/signified here merging with its correlative, or the sign, itself. The entire picture is framed by a vertical whisper of smoke from an ignited cigarette resting on an ashtray in the lower left-hand side of advertisement, connecting a corrugated frame at its head and foot. That smoke trail and those linear, willowy calligraphic forms—alongside the exaggerated flourish of the letter G of cigarros, and the 'de' of 'Son de El Buen Tono' in the advert's lower right hand side—speak to contemporary 'art deco' design (an international 'form of modern minimalism', Hammill and Smith 2015: 89) and also recall the shape of the very product being advertised, correlating aesthetic and product in their common, cosmopolitan modernity. The absence of any human figure and the cigarette's angle in the ashtray, which is positioned in the advert's outer frame, invite the participation of the reader/spectator: they point to an internal absence that 'anticipates the receiving subject' and also imply a narrative of some kind. The lit cigarette indicates the (albeit short-term) absence of a smoker (and raises a number of questions: 'Who are they?', 'Where have they gone?', 'What interrupted his/her smoking?'); it indicates an absence into which the

Fig. 3.2 Elegantes advertisement, *Mexican Folkways*, 3, 1927

reader can merge and take 'his' place (and, as I shall clarify below, it is likely to be a he), to savour that elegant, fine-tasting, smoke.

In other issues of *Folkways*, El Buen Tono's *Número 12* brand is promoted in similar terms, though in plainer half-page adverts, the largest font size of caption reserved for the brand name, followed by that of the manufacturing company: 'Todos los fumadores de buen gusto aseguran que [*El Número 12*] … es el mejor cigarro que se conoce' [All smokers of good taste agree that Number 12 is the best cigarette around] (In so far as they rely entirely on captions such advertisements might at first glance seem reminiscent of wholesale or trade advertisements, though it is likely that they speak to a pre-1930 preference for textual advertisements) (Fig. 3.3).

Once again, as in the case of the *Elegantes* advertisement, the emphasis is on the cigarette's high quality, on discernment and on the appellation of the reader as a unique and special individual, as already part of a clique of consumers with knowledge, good taste and propriety, the latter qualities crystallized in the tobacco company's own name, which was taken from an expression to refer to good familial pedigree and manners.[15] Though relatively economical in their visual language, to be sure, these advertisements yoke this cigarette brand to notions of leisure, sophistication, and style, portraying it, as Bunker puts it, 'as the ticket to a dream world of success for which most of their consumers could only puff and pray' (Bunker 1977: 237). That El Buen Tono cigarettes were marketed as abbreviated forms of diversion and respite is illuminating for, as Jackson Lears notes in his cultural history of advertising

Fig. 3.3 Número 12 advertisement, *Mexican Folkways*

in America, by comparison 'the pace of cigar smoking [which had long been linked with relaxation] began to seem too leisurely for the pattern of life promoted' (1994: 181) by advertisers in the early decades of the twentieth century. Indeed, in the late nineteenth century, as Susan Wagner documents, cigarettes started to appeal to 'a more prosperous and refined public than chewing tobacco and pipes had reached, or even cigars' (1971: 34). This was due in part to their attunement to the tempo and character of a growing urban population and culture north of the Mexico–US border: 'Tobacco supplied something romantic that was missing' (Wagner 1971: 34). El Buen Tono's adverts speak to a further issue of concern in Mexico, that is, the development of taste, which historically 'lagged behind the growth of wealth' (Johns 1997: 31). The cigarette manufacturer's name, branding, visual and rhetorical language all supply, in different but complementary ways, style, discernment, even good health (for while the phrase *buen tono* is best translated as 'good upbringing', *tono* can also mean tone).[16] The cigarettes' marketing as such to United States—and, importantly, also Mexican—consumers in the *Folkways* advertisements is belied by a fundamental irony, however: the qualities of respite and 'tonic' they offer in Mexico, a destination sought after by the tourist for the authenticity and exoticism (particularly) of its native peoples and history, were all under threat precisely from the very modernizing processes the country was also then embracing.

El Buen Tono's adverts and captions in *Folkways* are all in Spanish and, like many of the commercial advertisements published in the magazine, are relatively simple and 'unsophisticated' in their designs when compared with those published in other contemporary magazines of the era. This is not to say that the adverts in *Folkways* are innocent or unpersuasive in their rhetoric, for, as McFall argues, persuasiveness is 'not a function of any given element or combination of elements [of an advertisement] but … a historically contingent judgment' (McFall 2004: 154).[17] Rather it is to emphasize their distinctiveness in direct comparison with, say, the multitude of elaborate, eye-catching visual designs populating the pages of a popular weekly commercial title such as *Revista de revistas*. Nevertheless, in the context of El Buen Tono's credentials and extensive experience in publicity, the largely unadorned advertisements in *Folkways* seem anomalous. The cigarette manufacturer was at the vanguard of advertising, aesthetically and materially, and was unique in housing its own department of lithography, which became central in its efforts to promote its products. El Buen Tono's principal lithographer was Juan B. Urrutia who, from 1898 onwards, designed most of the company's publicity and packaging, as well as converted images from its cigarette packets into magazine advertising. The company even engaged the services of the avant-garde Estridentistas to design an original 1927 campaign for its Radio brand of cigarettes, which were duly depicted 'in a futuristic world filled with skyscrapers, neon lights, and machines' (Gallo 2005: 144).[18] The company's owner, Ernesto Pugibet, was mindful of the task he faced in promoting his products: in a country in which the elite consumer tended to favour imported cigars, and the mass consumer was used to cheap and readily available roll-your-own tobacco, he knew that to enter the market he needed to offer not only a modern, industrial product, but to associate it with values such as quality, hygiene, distinction, and aspiration: 'era necesario reforzar [los valores] a través de las imágenes de las cajetillas y una publicidad que difundiera de una manera accesible las cualidades extrínsecas e intrínsecas de los cigarros industriales' [It was necessary to reinforce (those values) through the images on packaging and advertising that disseminated accessibly the extrinsic and intrinsic qualities of industrial cigarettes] (Camacho Morfin and Pichardo 2006: 90). Rivalry with competitors such as La Tabacalera Mexicana during the so-called tobacco wars also galvanized Pugibet's marketing efforts.[19] In addition to its print campaigns, therefore, the company sponsored free cinema screenings, a lottery, a radio station and a dirigible, and published comic strips about ordinary life in Mexico in the daily newspapers, beginning in *El Imparcial* in 1904.[20] The spectacle of its dirigible's 1907 flights consolidated El Buen Tono's reputation for innovation and modernity, as Denise Hellion writes:

> Los recorridos [del dirigible] unían el espacio empresarial con el público multitudinario y ofrecían una visión del futuro. La empresa se colocaba en ese horizonte y los consumidores podían ser trasladados de su presente – convertido en un pasado rebasado por la modernidad – para compartir ese porvenir que estaba entre las nubes. (Hellion 2011: 19)

> [The (dirgible's) trips brought the business world and mass public together and offered a vision of the future. The company was situated on that horizon and consumers could be transferred from the present – converted into a past overtaken by modernity – to share in that future in the clouds.]

In this light, the *Elegantes* advertisement in *Folkways* seems deliberately anachronistic. Its 'art deco' font aside, that the image in that advertisement is a line drawing, rather than a photographic reproduction, underscores its own handmade, 'artistic' origins. This connection is seemingly at odds with both the (actual, more general) promotion of the product's modernity and the cigarette manufacturer's own history (to which I return below), as well as the magazine's prevailing interest in photography. Aesthetically, the obvious eschewal of a photographic image, which were in wide circulation and application in advertising at that time and in features elsewhere in the same magazine, in favour of the more time-intensive hand drawing, aligns the product with an economy of making. Indeed, if 'the technique of reproduction detaches the reproduced object from the domain of tradition' (Benjamin 1999: 215), the advert's reliance on the hand drawing rather than mass-manufactured photographic image fundamentally reattaches the cigarette to the kind of manually produced indigenous craft traditions and artisanal practices that are the predominant subject of interest elsewhere in *Folkways*. The advert's aesthetic insistence on the handmade and non-mechanical thus befogs the division between the artisanal and the commercial and implicitly aligns the product with other local productions depicted in the magazine (pottery, textiles, masks, jewellery), emblems all of Mexicanness in some way. At the same time, it invests this design and, by extension, the tobacco product with an aura of recreation, independence, and privilege. In this respect, the advertisement anticipates what Arjun Appadurai calls production fetishism, which rests on the illusion of romanticized forms of local production and national sovereignty. Depicting its brand(s) as consonant with the kind of tradition promulgated by *Folkways* and sought after by tourists visiting Mexico clearly serves the tobacco manufacturers' purpose: in this instance, El Buen Tono's tobacco product offers timeless, ineffable 'tradition' as respite from the rapid pace of Anglophone modernity, as well as a souvenir to recreate that experience back home.

In light of El Buen Tono's particular expertise in publicity as well as of the spectacular character of advertising, periodical, and the wider visual culture of that period (and, notwithstanding the company's long-standing dependence on lithography, that technical circumstances do not appear to have been a limiting factor at stake in this case), it is not unreasonable to deduce that the (extra)ordinary style of these adverts is a result of an accommodation to the agenda, objectives, and 'tone' of *Folkways* itself. *Folkways* was not a mass circulation publication, like *Revista de revistas*: it appealed to a literate audience and therefore advertisements carried in its pages did not need to rely on visual composition alone, though economic factors will also have been at play too. However, a more vivid, expressive promotional apparatus might have constituted a visual misdirection from the magazine's main features and 'serious' outlook, the professional photographic images of which might reasonably have curtailed the ambitions of a staff artist in El Buen Tono's employ. It is noteworthy that, in comparison, other contemporary 'little' magazines in Mexico at this time carried either little or no advertising, or had advertising specifically tailoured to their readerships, while populist publications such as *Revista de revistas* were replete with them. The literary magazine *México moderno*, for example, which ran from 1920 to 1923, published notices only for itself, other germane magazines (e.g. *Revista musical de México*), Steinway pianos, and classifieds for professional music teachers, or for a limited range of what were then deemed modern national goods, including beer (Toluca Extra and Victoria) and gasoline (Naftolina).[21] There is more to say about the implications of El Buen Tono's advertisements in this chapter's concluding section.

The Hotel Genève was another regular advertiser in the pages of *Mexican Folkways*. If cigarettes provide an example of a common (so-called search) good, by contrast hotels are one of a number of 'experience' goods, that is, goods that cannot be inspected before purchase and thus rely on reputation and trust as firm-specific assets ('the essence of the product is, in fact', as Michael Clancy puts it, 'the quality of that experience', 2001: 71).[22] Notwithstanding significant differences from the previous example as a 'commodity', hotels are of central importance in the experience of tourism and among its primary beneficiaries; as such, they are major sites of investment and construction and major advertisers in the sector. Moreover, hotels, as George F. Flaherty points out, insofar as they house 'the many contradictions of modernity's "transcendental homelessness"', have a symbolic relationship to the nation: in Mexico they have become an emblem of the single-party modernizing authoritarian state 'that claimed the role of absolute host and treated most of its citizens as mere guests, with only limited rights and few alternatives' (Flaherty 2016: 99, 103). The Hotel Genève was characterized in travel guides of the 1920s and 1930s as 'thoroughly modern (the largest in Mexico)'. It was 'strictly American (American ownership, management and cooking)', 'in one of the healthiest sections of the city' in Liverpool, in the *zona rosa*, constructed 'of concrete and steel (fire and earthquake proof)' and 'much liked for its many refinements' (Terry 1923: 234). Anita Brenner, in her popular guidebook *Your Mexican Holiday*, described the Hotel Genève as a luxurious, upper scale hotel, 'very large, kept constantly modern' by its owner Thomas Gore, with one of its main features being the 'lavish colonial note in furnishings' (Brenner 1932: 383). In early issues of *Folkways*, plain script advertisements for the hotel underscored many of these features: its independent, American ownership—the *Folkways* advertisement naming the hotel specifically as the *American* Hotel Genève ('First in size and quality'), a shift in title from a contemporaneous edition of the renowned *Terry's Guide* where it was listed as a more European-sounding Hotel *de* Genève. In either iteration, with or without the modifier or preposition, the hotel's designation speaks to its avowedly bicultural identity, the building's hybrid architectural composition and décor as well as the business's market ambitions as a New World conception of Old World style. The emphasis in *Folkways* on its American 'identity' indicates to the magazine's Anglophone readership not only ownership but familiarity and trust in the already known and experienced. In later issues of the magazine, from 1929 onwards, the hotel's advertisements began to carry photographic images of its interior and exterior, as in Fig. 3.4, which underscored this gesture of recognition.

Notable here, as in the previous example of the *Elegantes* cigarettes advert, is the inclusion of captions and the absence of human figures, in this case in a side-angled photograph of the hotel lobby, which visually

Fig. 3.4 Hotel Genève advertisement, *Mexican Folkways*, 3:1, 1927, p. 1

captures its voluminous proportions and generous interior space. In underlining its 'American comforts' and potential for familiar leisure activities such as tennis, the advert's captions, like the photograph, work to contain risk; promoting known sporting pastimes as well as recognized spatial arrangements was and remains important for tourists in an unfamiliar environment such as a foreign country (Clancy 2001: 74). However, the camera's point of view sets up a dynamic, forward-moving trajectory, redolent of a classic modernist/futurist perspective, but symbolic also of the aspirations of the industry the advert promotes.

In one of the last issues of *Mexican Folkways*, volume 8 (1937), a special number on the Yaquí Indians, two half-page photographs of the hotel's façade and lobby dominate a striking full-page advertisement (the only full page advert ever printed in the magazine), in prime location on the issue's first page, after the inside front cover (Fig. 3.5).

Captions in a broad, clean sans serif font celebrate the hotel's recent expansion to 450 rooms, bathrooms, and garage and underscore the hotel's superlative size and significance, as the 'largest and most important [hotel] south of the Rio Grande'. Each of this advertisement's photographs, unpopulated by human characters with the exception of two barely discernible figures at the hotel's entrance in the upper image, provide expansive, frontal views of the building's vast proportions and fabric. The focus on the hotel's obviously concrete construction highlights its modernity, for as Gallo explains, as an inexpensive and modern building material, cement, like photography, gained popularity as another 'new' technology during the 1920s. It was regarded as 'efficient and

Fig. 3.5 Hotel Genève advertisement, *Mexican Folkways*, 9:1, 1937, p. 1

forward-looking', a building material that articulated a clear break with the [marble-dominated] architecture of the *Porfiriato*, and soon became 'the perfect substance for building the new Mexico envisioned by the postrevolutionary government' (Gallo 2005: 172).

The neat geometric lines of the hotel's architectural design and its modern construction materials are thrown into relief, however, by other details in both images: trees and plants placed in linear arrangements on the pavement outside the hotel's entrance and in strategic patterns in the vestibule and mezzanine of its interior, which is in turn furnished with heavy, colonial-style wooden tables and chairs. As Krista Thomson points out in another context, in the tourist industry such an instance of or a gesture towards 'tropicalisation' (here, in flora and furnishings), based on reconstructions of the country's past, in fact became more broadly a 'forward-looking project for ... [post-colonial] elites' (2006: 12–15), valued paradoxically for the modernity it could bring about in terms of attracting tourists and their capital. In contrast to the fussyness of the historic 1929 image of the hotel on its website, where the ornate carvings of the vestibule's columns, abundant plants and intricate glass details connote more typical and abundant tropical elegance, the full-page advertisement in *Folkways* is more sparse and vacant and emanates a futuristic quality.[23] That is, the tropical, neo-colonial revival is contained, while the solidity and orderliness of the modern architectural design and construction promise class, style, and consolation to the foreign tourist.[24] That advertisement's tamed and domesticated version of nature and tradition indicates to potential tourists safety, discipline, and order in the foreign environment: in effect, to draw further on Thomson's suggestions in the germane setting of the Caribbean, this is a 'visual treatment of the effectiveness of colonial rule and naturalized colonial and imperial transformations of social and physical landscape' (2006: 7). The vacancy of that image of the hotel, like the absence of the smoker from the El Buen Tono advert, also betokens a potential narrative, beckoning an implied reader/tourist in a search of 'authentic' experience but clean, modern accommodation. Though it is true that vacancy of a similar sort featured in much contemporary modernist photography of Mexico City (an urban landscape, Tenorio Trillo claims, that when photographed seemed devoid of people or only ever populated by poor brown bodies), in this tourism advertisement that absence has a particular freight.[25] The advertisement, like a blank slate, invites the reader to occupy a place in the hotel's empty spaces, including its 'delightful lobby', which is devoid of other residents, staff, or any undesirable elements. The historic associations of other visual representations of blank spaces, such as those on maps for example, with (colonialist) expansion and incursion are also resonant here (for more on which, see Chapter 3). Yet, the vacancy is also redolent of a fundamental illusion: that is, the lobby offers 'only simulacra of unity and reconciliation' (Flaherty 2016: 106) for 'the togetherness in the hotel lobby has no meaning' (Kracauer 1999: 291). Although this advertisement's aesthetic choices are at odds with those of the retroactive hand-drawn adverts for El Buen Tono cigarettes, the implications are commensurate. The modern medium of photography, in which *Folkways* was so invested and ardently promoted, is critical to this: 'serving [itself] as a form of discipline', photography selected what was fit to be represented and 'offer[ed] an additional degree of assurance to travellers that "the natives" and the landscape were tamed, safe, and framed for their visual [ultimately material] consumption' (Thomson 2006: 17).

The coupling of cultural 'authenticity' with a 'first-world' hospitality experience has long been a consideration for designers and architects in Mexico: indeed, as Luis M. Castañeda points out, the standards for hotel design were set precisely in the 1930s, more or less contemporaneously with the publication of the *Folkways* advertisements for the Genève discussed here. Those design standards were established by the Mexican Automobilists Association (AMA), one of the country's earliest tourist associations, which 'called for simultaneous inclusion of "traditional" and "cosmopolitan" cultural references' in hotel construction (Castañeda 2014: 175). An adjacent advertisement on the same page of that issue of *Folkways* for the San Angel Inn reiterates that incongruous juxtaposition (see Fig. 3.4). A more traditional architectural and geographical prospect than the Genève, as it was converted from an old mission-style convent in the outskirts of Mexico City, the San Angel Inn advert (here as in other issues of the magazine) relies on captions to promote similar qualities. The tropical, exotic, and exclusive are recalled in references to the hotel's cuisine, elegance, and 'delightful old gardens' while its simultaneous modernity is addressed in the announcement of a European plan (where for the tourists' convenience the payment was for room and breakfast only, with other meals to be taken outside at extra cost) and articulated visually through the use of a contemporary font for the advert's lettering (Fig. 3.5).

III

What can such advertisements tell us about *Mexican Folkways* and, more broadly, Mexico during that dynamic period of nation-building after the Revolution? First, that the magazine took commercial advertising tells us something about Toor's ambitions and pragmatism as an editor. While she may have boasted about the magazine's independence—that it was published in Mexico City 'without any subsidy from a folklore society or rich benefactor'—the SEP subsidy was precarious. Commercial advertising enabled an additional income stream (it no doubt contributed to an increase in size and page numbers, as well as better quality paper in later issues), but even in an era where the relationship between the intellectual and state was close, albeit still unpredictable, it will also have betokened precious editorial autonomy. Second, if adverts for hotels, newsagents, and souvenir shops were targeted more obviously to tourists north of the border, the cigarette adverts also help us understand something more specific about the magazine's 'national' readership, notwithstanding the 'impossibility' of historical reconstruction of origins in this respect.[26] Of the many brands produced by El Buen Tono, the two promoted in *Folkways*—*El Número 12* and *Elegantes*—were specifically conceived for and marketed to young middle-upper class urban male consumers, a detail that gives us a clearer idea of the identity of (some of) the magazine's implied audience in and outside Mexico, one which is consonant with the shifts in tobacco consumption identified by Wagner to which I referred earlier. Third, alongside the magazine's dissemination of the country's folkways and indigenous cultures, the advertisements in *Folkways* depicted Mexico City as a cosmopolitan place of progress and modernity; a lettered city, with refrigeration, safe and comfortable accommodation, ample opportunities for consumerism, property development, and investment. Such marketing might have been at odds with the periodical's promotion of the country's unique rich ethnic and folkloric diversity, but it spoke acutely to Mexico's geopolitical aspirations. In short, in many ways these advertisements distilled one of the central fantasies of the Revolution, pithily summed up by Horacio Legrás: that 'the whole past was open to appropriation and the whole future to construction' (2017: 123).

Cigarettes and hotels provide instructive case studies of goods that were marketed precisely in seemingly dichotomous but overlapping terms of 'tradition' and 'modernity'. Moreover, their histories as goods speak to a revival or continuity of processes, stakeholders, and rhetoric that had been fundamental to nation-building during the *Porfiriato* in Mexico's post-revolutionary reconstruction. One of the ironies of the association between *Folkways* and El Buen Tono, for example, stems from the company's own transnational history. One of the most long-established tobacco companies in Mexico, El Buen Tono became well known for its French-style cigarettes and for its pioneering modernization of cigarette manufacturing. The company grew from humble, artisanal beginnings to become one of the largest enterprises in the country, a rise due in part to its political connections both under Díaz and post-revolutionary governments. Indeed, El Buen Tono was considered 'un modelo del ideal porfiriano del progreso' [of model of the Porfirian ideal of progress] (Camacho Morfin and Pichardo 2006: 89): Díaz attended the opening ceremony of the company's second site in May 1897, as did the opera singer Emma Calve in 1908, after whom it named one of its lines, and Porfirio Díaz Jr. sat on its board of directors (Haber 1989: 100). In its seventy-seven years of operation, El Buen Tono manufactured dozens of different cigarette brands, among them Héroe de la paz, a line conceived in homage to, and with an image on its packaging of, Díaz.[27] The company's founder, the Frenchman Pugibet, whose residence in Cuba equipped him with the necessary expertise about the cultivation of tobacco and cigarette production, migrated to Mexico in 1879, it is thought, in response to Mexican government efforts at that time to attract foreign investors to participate in the country's development. Financed by a substantial family inheritance bequeathed to his Mexican wife, Guadalupe Portilla, who also worked in the company in its early days, Pugibet introduced new technology to cigarette manufacturing in Mexico, which also enabled his company's monopoly of the industry for many years. For example, in 1885 he patented machines to package cigarettes more rapidly and in 1889 introduced into his factory Decloufé machinery, which effectively brought the cigarette's traditional handmade manufacture to an end. By the end of that year, Pugibet's factory was producing over three and a half million cigarettes daily. Indeed, that this 'undisputed giant of the cigarette industry' effectively quashed small-scale artisan cigarette production in Mexico illuminates the material as well as ideological paradox of its hand-drawn aesthetic in the *Folkways* advertisement discussed above, which exalted the handmade and the local just as (or indeed even because) the company was modernizing and internationalizing at such an expeditious rate (Haber 1989: 100). A business founded by a European trained in Cuba, funded by Mexican money, and facilitated by French technological innovations, El Buen Tono became an international success, its products and promotional campaigns winning various overseas competitions, and it was appointed as official supplier to the Spanish royal household in 1908.[28] The notions of modernity and leisure on which it traded, as seen in the discussion earlier, as well as the concern for hygiene (also advertising its *Charros* brand in *Folkways*, for example, as 'suaves y agradables al más refinado fumador … higiénicos, engargolados sin pegamento' [smooth and pleasant for the most refined smoker… hygienic, sealed without adhesive], 4:2, 1928, 76), were also all fundamental ideals of the Porfirian era that were nonetheless being rehearsed and recodified in the new Republic.[29]

The Hotel Genève's history is similarly telling in terms of the transnational and trans-historical interplay that underpinned Mexico's postrevolutionary reconstruction, and which, 'challenges the way [we] normally conceive of foreign and national and imperialism and cultural sovereignty' (López 2010: 97). The hotel was modelled, as its name suggests, after the tradition of grand European hotels. It opened in 1907, in which year it was first photographed by the renowned German-Mexican photographer Guillermo Kahlo. Boasting a close connection with major historical events in Mexico, it was at the Hotel Genève where President Díaz dined with his family on the day that the Revolution broke out on 20 November 1910. The hotel continues to underscore its reputation as 'a constant innovator in the Mexican tourist industry', reaching back to its inception: it was the first hotel to admit unaccompanied single women as well as the first hotel in Mexico to offer a taxi service, telephone switchboard operators, dry cleaning, a travel agency, elevators, as well as a bathroom in every room. Indeed, by 1930, the Hotel Genève was the only hotel in Mexico City considered to be first class, and 'thus satisfactory for American tourists' (Terry 1923: 235), by Frank Dudley, president of the United States Hotels Company of America, though he still regarded it then in need of extensive renovation. Thomas Gore, 'an experienced hotel manager of international repute' (Berger 2006: 41), refurbished the hotel in 1931, adding 180 rooms to the original 120 and installing en-suite bathrooms in all the rooms. As Dina Berger notes, Gore requested a tax exemption from the government on the materials he imported from the United States for that purpose (Berger 2006: 135). Gore himself was part of the American colony that had first settled in Mexico during the *Porfiriato* and went on to become a member of a group of influential American developers and bankers that, during a wave of rapid construction in the capital at the turn of the nineteenth and twentieth centuries, 'mobilized local capital to push Mexico City beyond its colonial limits for the first time' (Schell 2001: 53). Gore, for example, built some of Mexico City's earliest apartments, Gore Courts and Gore Place, and he was a founding board member of the AMA, the group that set the standards for hotel design and construction for decades to come (Berger 2006: 51). Indeed, in many ways, the Hotel Genève's promotion in *Folkways* anticipates the kind of issues that would dominate the construction of Mexico City hotels during the capital's fateful hosting of the 1968 Olympics. Then, tradition and modernity, authenticity and cosmopolitan hospitality, came into dialogue once again in Ricardo Legoretta's design for the Camino Real Hotel, an important convention centre for Olympic diplomatic events and host of prominent international visitors, among them the International Olympic Committee (IOC) President (Castañeda 2014: 176). In this instance, the hotel cited tradition rather than modernity in its building materials, Legoretta opting, instead of cement, for sun-dried brick in its construction, 'a material used in pre-Columbian, colonial and modern-day "vernacular" buildings in several regions of Mexico' (Castañeda 2014: 179) and rough plaster walls in the hotel's common areas. As in the Hotel Genève thirty years earlier, however, the Camino Real's décor included replicas and originals of colonial candlesticks and dressers, which 'contrasted in jarring ways with the fully abstract forms of the hotel's interior' as well as the use of artworks by the internationally renowned Rufino Tamayo, 'Mexico's most sought after official painter', who drew on pre-Hispanic and folk-art traditions in his work (Castañeda 2014: 175, 181).[30]

To be sure, there is ample evidence in *Mexican Folkways* of what Shelley Garrigan, in her study of monuments and museums in nineteenth-century Mexico City, calls the 'dialectical embrace of patrimony and market', the latter a value system, she cautions, that 'presents a potential threat to a community that is still in the process of defining itself', not least to Mexico during its protracted process of nation-building after the Revolution. Yet, as Garrigan observes, and as the advertising in *Folkways* illustrates in unique ways, 'the commercial subtext of Mexican patrimony was integral to the emerging national profile and in fact anticipated the negotiations that regional and national guardians of cultural patrimony would face in the context of globalization in the century to follow' (Garrigan 2012: 123). *Mexican Folkways* functioned as a guide to the 'new' Republic for domestic and international readers alike; its editor and contributors, likewise, were cast as 'modern discoverers of an unknown country'. In addition to constituting the kind of archival collection of Mexico's art, legends, and folklore that Toor had envisaged, the magazine functioned in certain ways as a catalogue of said traditions and the country's native peoples, but also of available goods and services.

To address this latter aspect of *Folkways* is not an attempt to diminish the magazine's significance; rather, to redeem it from its prevailing function as mere source material, 'strip-mined' solely for discrete pieces of information or treated only for particular historiographical interest, rather than studied as a composite aesthetic or cultural object in its own right. Indeed, if one of the shortcomings of folkloric studies and endeavours (such as *Folkways* itself) is that 'cultural goods - objects, legends, musical forms - are of greater interest than the actors who generate and consume them' and thus 'always a melancholic attempt at subtracting the popular from the massive reorganization of society' (García Canclini 1995: 151), then arguably *Mexican Folkways* has been subject in turn to an analogous procedure by scholars, who have neglected the processes and agents involved in its creation, in favour of a fascination with the periodical as product and source. This chapter has proposed reading *Mexican Folkways* as an 'autonomous' object of study, through an engagement with its visual *and* discursive material (and the interplay between their constituent parts, as discussed above) but also with its narrative trajectory, or, as discussed in the first section, the magazine's own biography over a lifetime in print. To that end, this chapter has marshalled a multi-method approach corresponding to the complexity of the material at hand in order to bring to light the magazine's hitherto unstudied paratextual features and to apprehend advertising as part of Mexico's broader visual culture and history. If the preceding discussion has illuminated the porosity of boundaries between national and transnational conceptualizations of culture and the less than clear-cut divisions between pre-and post-revolutionary Mexico, the periodical has transpired to be an exemplary expression of the difficulties entailed in separating out different epochs, nations, media, and value systems. Horacio Legrás's reading of the Revolution in terms of textuality offers a useful conceptual framework in this respect. Acknowledging the ever-expanding archive of/on Revolutionary Mexico (of which this book forms part), he argues that an understanding of the Revolution as textuality allows 'the element of contiguity precedence over previous forms of relationship based on hierarchies' since 'in revolution, works, people and ideas are not contained by firm and established boundaries [but] enter into unexpected conjunctions and borrowings' (Legrás 2017: 3). As a miscellany of material in discontinuous form, the magazine visually and materially choreographs that very conception of textuality. Indeed, if one of the much-lauded innovations of *Mexican Folkways* was its presentation in content of the 'real' Mexico as rural and indigenous (in chorus with nationalist ideas of the period), at the same time its commercial associations and engagement with the 'new science' of advertising also grounded the magazine firmly in urban modernity and implicated it fully in the business of shaping Mexico's consumer-citizens and tourists in and outside of the new Republic.

Notes

1. For more on this see Scarles (2009) and Hummon (1988).
2. See Thacker (2010) and Scholes and Wulfman (2010: 118–142).
3. McFall questions the validity of a purely semiotic approach to advertisements in her work. Acknowledging the critical fascination with adverts and what they have to reveal about societies, cultures, and economies, she asks whether it is 'really adequate to found a critique that reaches far into the nature and organization of contemporary societies upon textual deconstruction of the meanings of advertisements?' (3). In turn, Sinervo and Hill concur with the need to consider the economic and political factors at stake in visual representations of tourism from an ethnographic perspective, in order to avoid falling into the trap of 'predictable' essentialist identity politics (Sinervo and Hill 2011: 127).
4. As Erica Segre has pointed out, the articulation of national narratives did not necessarily sit easily with different presiding governments' ideologies over that period, or necessarily coincide with the views of 'a mobilized, patriotic public': 'Nor did the intellectual or artistic community coalesce behind the banner of the civic-minded, declamatory aesthetic and exclusivity of an enabling *mexicanismo*', she observes (Segre 2007: 88).
5. As Legrás observes, the state 'borrowed the eyes of painters like Francisco Goitia in the excavation of Teotihuacán or the eyes of a Rivera in the dissemination of its own credo through popular and rural education' (2017: 11).

6. Mobile teacher training units called cultural missions travelled to rural villages, established libraries and trained teachers. A system of rural secondary schools that provided room and board, education and training free of cost was also established by the Ministry of Education (SEP). Other educational initiatives included the publication of cheap editions of canonical books of the Western tradition, which were placed in small libraries throughout the Republic. By late 1925 there were more than 3000 libraries and over 200 federal rural primary schools, a system that continued to expand into the 1930s by which time (1936), there were more than 11,000 rural schools. A department of fine arts was established to encourage the plastic arts, music, and literature and artists such as José Clemente Orozco and Diego Rivera were commissioned to paint public murals, which glorified a multiethnic nation (Beezley and Meyers 2010: 450–453).
7. For more on this see Delpar (1992). Gamio studied under Boas at Columbia University and became his protégé, his time in New York 'coincid[ing] with a period of enthusiasm for Mexican archaeology and anthropology on the part of Boas' (Delpar 1992: 97). Boas's belief in the unity of indigenous New World cultures was a critical factor in his interest in Mexico and led to the establishment of the shortlived International School of American Archaeology and Ethnology in 1911. Toor herself claimed not to be a scholar but to be interested above all in contributing to a greater understanding of Mexico in the rest of the world. In a letter of December 1932 to the anthropologist Elsie Clews Parsons, she indicated that 'I'm more than content to have won the respect of people like you, Dr. [Franz] Boas, Dr. Paul Rivet and others for folkways' (cited in http://www.encyclopedia.com/women/encyclopedias-almanacs-transcripts-and-maps/toor-frances-1890-1956, accessed 22 March 2017). For more on Franz Boas and his legacy, see Maxwell (2012), Lévy Zumwalt (2013), and Whitfield (2010).
8. For a complete index of the magazine's content, see Boggs (1945).
9. The nature of that collaboration began to change from the 1930s onwards, due to anxieties about US expansionism during the interwar years and the increase in US researchers' activity elsewhere in the world (López 2010: 122).
10. See Johns (1997).
11. In cultural relations between the United States and Mexico after 1920, art was the most attractive aspect of postrevolutionary Mexico. Not only were all forms of Mexican artistic production exhibited and generally well received in the US, but, as Delpar observes, they were also rooted in the history and popular culture of Mexico: 'the Mexicans seemed to have

created what many members of the American art world were seeking: an authentically national mode of art' (1992: 125).
12. The National Agricultural Credit Bank was established by President Calles in 1926, 'most of whose funds were absorbed by large landowners in the north', among them the Sonoran chickpea farmer and later president Alvaro Obregón. It was reorganized in 1931 to assist cooperative societies made up of *ejidos* and small farmers and it extended credit to cooperatives for the purchase of seed, fertilizer, and farm machinery (Beezley and Meyer 2010: 461).
13. As John Sinclair points out, 'national' advertisers are so-called 'because of their capacity to produce, distribute and advertise their brands throughout a whole country [not because] they are "national" companies: many in fact will be found to be subsidiaries of the transnational or "multinational" companies … such as Ford or [Unilever]' (1989: 4). Anne Rubenstein identifies four 'broad and overlapping' categories of advertisement during this period: direct translations of advertisements from foreign publications; those for products associated with revolutionary nationalism; those that referred to modernity in terms of technological progress; and those for products associated with racial or regional pride (2010: 602–603).
14. As Susan Wagner points out, tobacco is 'a purely American plant', its smoking originating in the coastal regions of Central and South America: 'the oldest known evidence of tobacco use is found on a Mayan stone carving at Palenque [Chiapas] … in a bas-relief representing a priest blowing smoke through a long tube' (Wagner 1971: 6). On cigarettes as luxury commodities, see Williamson (1978: 32–39). For more on alcohol in Mexico, see Toner (2015).
15. As Gallo points out: 'El Buen Tono was named after an old-fashioned expression, immensely popular during the *Porfiriato*, that is best translated as "good upbringing" and was used to refer to the impeccable manners and flawless social etiquette that was expected of "good families" in prerevolutionary Mexico' (2005: 143).
16. See Gallo (2005: 143).
17. McFall helpfully advises against falling into the trap of considering adverts of the past as qualitatively different to those of the contemporary period, as having only a function to inform, rather than persuade (2004: 153–154).
18. El Buen Tono subsequently 'effectively became their corporate patron' (Gallo 2005: 146). For more on this, see Gallo (2005: 141–156).
19. For more on this see Bunker (1977: 237).
20. See https://cinesilentemexicano.wordpress.com/2012/05/28/la-compania-cigarrera-de-el-buen-tono-y-el-cine-la-calle-de-mayo-28-2012/ (accessed 14 June 2016)

21. As Thacker points out, advertisements for other magazines and for publishers 'were often accepted on a "no cost" or mutual basis' and as a result 'did not bring in revenue as such' (2010: 7).
22. In Mexico, prior to WWII, the period of our concern, hotel owners and operators were mostly independent (many small and family-run) operations, until the arrival in the 1940s of pioneers such as Intercontinental and Hilton.
23. http://www.hotelgeneve.com.mx/en/hotel-geneve/#prettyPhoto (accessed 26 July 2016).
24. If in 1932 Brenner drew attention to the colonial décor of the Hotel (de) Genève, it continues to exalt its classical European style on its present website: 'Our guests, while strolling the hotel, will discover interesting antiques and works of art that have been part of the history of this unique "museum hotel"'. See http://www.hotelgeneve.com.mx/en/ (accessed 26 July 2016).
25. See Tenorio Trillo (2012: 168–207).
26. The difficulty in reconstructing readerships is, as Will Straw has pointed out, due to the absence of 'tokens' such as advertisements, letters to the editor, or other references in popular culture to the reading of periodicals, which normally serve to specify readers. Quoted in Hammill et al. (2015: 8).
27. El Buen Tono's brands included Reina Victoria, Alfonso XIII, Country Club, Jazz, Campeones (for sportsmen), Canela Pura and Margaritas (for women). It made cigarettes for export to markets in Europe (e.g. La Parisienne) as well as for the mass audience (La Popular and Mascota), and it even produced a line of chocolate cigarettes for children, for the consumers of the future.
28. In the late 1920s, however, after two decades of unparalleled success, the company suffered the effects of the world silver and oil crises, and for the first time in its history registered financial losses, so that it did not pay a dividend to shareholders. Increased competition from rivals such as El Aguila, which had been founded in 1926 with plants in Mexico City and Guanajuato, and a new taste for blonde tobacco products from North America also meant the start of a rapid loss of market share for El Buen Tono. As Stephen Haber points out, the company 'either lost money or earned very little in every year between 1932 and 1937 ... losses [which] were less than they had been during the late 1920s, when losses equalled 10–13% of capital stock per year' (Haber 1989: 182). El Buen Tono was eventually bought by Tabacalera Mexicana in 1961. For more on the company's economic history see Haber, *Industry and Underdevelopment*, *passim*.
29. As Ricardo López-León has pointed out, hygiene became equated with modernity in illustrated advertising in print media after the Revolution.

In 'Science and Technology as Key Shapers of Modernity: Illustrated Advertising in Mexican Magazines and Newspapers (1920–1960)', Paper delivered as SLAS annual conference, Birkbeck, University of London, April 2015. See also López-León (2009).
30. That building's low-rise layout, dominated by strong colours from a typical Mexican palette, was also redolent of 'the planning principles of colonial-period haciendas and of monastic architecture more generally' (Castañeda 2014: 180).

References

Albiñana, Salvador. 2010. *Mexico ilustrado: libros, revistas y carteles 1920–1950*. Mexico: Editorial RM.

Beezley, William H., and Michael C. Meyer, eds. 2010. *The Oxford History of Mexico*. New York: Oxford University Press.

Benjamin, Walter. 1999. *Illuminations*. London: Pimlico.

Benjamin, Thomas. 2010. 'Rebuilding the Nation.' In *The Oxford History of Mexico*, edited by William H. Beezley and Michael C. Meyer, 438–470. New York: Oxford University Press.

Berger, Dina. 2006. *The Development of Mexico's Tourism Industry: Pyramids by Day, Martinis by Night*. New York: Palgrave Macmillan.

Boggs, Ralph Steele. 1945. *Bibliografía completa, clasificada y comentada de los artículos de Mexican Folkways, con índice*. Mexico City: Instituto Panamericano de Geografía e Historia.

Brenner, Anita. 1932. *Your Mexican Holiday*. New York: Putnams.

Bunker, Steven B. 1977. 'Consumers of Good Taste: Marketing Modernity in North Mexico 1890–1910.' *Mexican Studies/Estudios Mexicanos* 3 (2): 227–269.

Camacho Morfin, Thelma, and Hugo Pichardo. 2006. 'La cigarrera El Buen Tono (1889–1929).' In *Poder público y poder privado: gobierno, empresarios y empresas 1880–1980*, edited by José Mario Contreras Valdez and Jesús Méndez Reyes, 83–106. Mexico: UNAM.

Castañeda, Luis M. 2014. *Spectacular Mexico: Design, Propaganda, and the 1968 Olympics*. Minneapolis: University of Minnesota Press.

Clancy, Michael. 2001. *Exporting Paradise: Tourism and Development in Mexico*. Amsterdam: Pergamon.

Delpar, Helen. 1992. *The Enormous Vogue of Things Mexican: Cultural Relationships Between the US and Mexico 1920–1935*. Tuscaloosa: University of Alabama Press.

Elizalde, Lydia, ed. 2007. *Revistas culturales latinoamericanas 1920–1960*. Mexico City: CONACULTA.

Feighey, William. 2003. 'Negative Image? Developing the Visual in Tourism Research.' *Current Issues in Tourism* 6 (1): 76–85.

Flaherty, George F. 2016. *Hotel Mexico: Dwelling on the '68 Movement*. Oakland: University of California Press.

Gallo, Ruben. 2005. *Mexican Modernity: The Avant-Garde and the Technological Revolution*. Cambridge: MIT Press.

García Canclini, Nestor. 1995. *Hybrid Cultures: Strategies for Entering and Leaving Modernity*. Translated by Christopher L. Chiappari and Silvia L. López. Minneapolis and London: University of Minnesota Press.

Garrigan, Shelley E. 2012. *Collecting Mexico: Museums, Monuments, and the Creation of National Identity*. Minneapolis: University of Minnesota Press.

Haber, Stephen. 1989. *Industry and Underdevelopment: The Industrialization of Mexico 1890–1940*. Stanford: Stanford University Press.

Hammill, Faye, and Michelle Smith. 2015. *Magazines, Travel and Middlebrow Culture: Canadian Periodicals in English and French 1925–1960*. Liverpool: Liverpool University Press.

Hammill, Faye, Paul Hjartarson, and Hannah McGregor. 2015. 'Introducing Magazines and/as Media: The Aesthetics and Politics of Serial Form.' *ESC: English Studies in Canada* 41 (1): 1–18.

Hellion, Denise. 2011. 'Y la ciudad miró al cielo. El globo dirigible de El Buen Tono.' *Diario de Campo* 4: 1–19.

Hummon, David. 1988. 'Tourist Worlds: Tourist Advertising, Ritual, and American Culture.' *The Sociological Quarterly* 29 (2): 179–202.

Johns, Michael. 1997. *The City of Mexico in the Age of Díaz*. Austin: University of Texas Press.

Kitch, Caroline. 2005. *Pages From the Past: History and Memory in American Magazines*. Chapel Hill: University of North Carolina.

Kracauer, Siegfried. 1999. 'The hotel lobby'. *Postcolonial Studies* 2(3): 289–297.

Lears, Jackson. 1994. *Fables of Abundance: A Cultural History of Advertising in America*. New York: Basic.

Leed, Eric. 1992. *The Mind of the Traveller: From Gilgamesh to Global Tourism*. New York: Basic.

Legrás, Horacio. 2017. *Culture and Revolution: Violence, Memory, and the Making of Modern Mexico*. Austin: University of Texas Press.

Lévy Zumwalt, Rosemary. 2013. 'The Shaping of Intellectual Identity and Discipline Through Charismatic Leaders: Franz Boas and Alan Dundes.' *Western Folklore* 72 (2): 131–179.

López, Rick A. 2010. *Crafting Mexico: Intellectuals, Artisans, and the State After Revolution*. Durham: Duke University Press.

López-León, Ricardo. 2009. 'La ciencia y la tecnología como tópicas de la publicidad gráfica en la prensa de 1922 en México.' *Pensar la Publicidad* 3 (1): 219–238.

Maxwell, Anne. 2012. 'Modern Anthropology and the Problem of the Racial Type: The Photographs of Franz Boas.' *Visual Communication* 12 (1): 123–142.

McFall, Liz. 2004. *Advertising: A Cultural Economy*. London: Sage.

Mirzoeff, Nicolas. 2015. *How to See the World*. London: Penguin.

Moreno, Julio. 2003. *Yankee Don't Go Home! Mexican Nationalism, American Business Culture, and the Shaping of Modern Mexico, 1920–1950*. Chapel Hill: University of North Carolina Press.

Rogal, Maria. 2012. 'Identity and Representation: The (Yucatec) Maya in the Visual Culture of Tourism.' *Latin American and Caribbean Ethnic Studies* 7 (1): 49–69.

Rubenstein, Anne. 2010. 'Mass Media and Popular Culture in the Postrevolutionary Era.' In *The Oxford History of Mexico*, edited by William H. Beezley and Michael C. Meyer, 598–634. New York: Oxford University Press.

Scarles, Caroline. 2009. 'Becoming Tourist: Renegotiating the Visual in the Tourist Experience.' *Environment and Planning D: Society and Space* 27 (3): 465–488.

Schell, William. 2001. *Integral Outsiders: The American Colony in Mexico City 1876–1911*. Wilmington, Delaware: Scholarly Resources.

Scholes, Robert, and Clifford Wulfman. 2010. *Modernism in the Magazines: An Introduction*. New Haven and London: Yale University Press.

Segre, Erica. 2007. *Intersected Identities: Strategies of Visualization in 19th and 20th Century Mexican Culture*. London: Berghahn.

Sinclair, John. 1989. *Images Incorporated: Advertising as Industry and Ideology*. London and New York: Routledge.

Sinervo, Aviva, and Michael D. Hill. 2011. 'The Visual Economy of Andean Childhood Poverty: Interpreting Postcards in Cusco, Peru.' *The Journal of Latin American and Cultural Anthropology* 16 (1): 114–142.

Tenorio Trillo, Mauricio. 2012. *I Speak of the City: Mexico at the Turn of the 20th Century (1880–1940)*. Chicago: University of Chicago Press.

Terry, T. Phillip. 1923. *Terry's Guide to Mexico: The New Standard Guidebook to the Mexican Republic*. Boston: Houghton Mifflin.

Thacker, Andrew. 2010. 'Modern Tastes in Rhythm: The Visual and Verbal Culture of Advertisement of Modernist Magazines.' *Katherine Mansfield Studies* 2: 4–19.

Thomson, Krista. 2006. *An Eye for the Tropics: Tourism, Photography, and Framing the Caribbean Picturesque*. Durham: Duke University Press.

Toner, Deborah. 2015. *Alcohol and Nationhood in Nineteenth-Century Mexico*. Lincoln and London: University of Nebraska Press.

Wagner, Susan. 1971. *Cigarette Country: Tobacco in American History and Politics*. New York: Praeger.

White, Cameron, John L. Oliffe, and Joan L. Bottorff. 2012. 'From the Physician to the Marlboro Man: Masculinity, Health, and Cigarette Advertising in America, 1946–1964.' *Men and Masculinities* 15 (5): 526–547.

Whitfield, Stephen. 2010. 'Franz Boas: The Anthropologist as Public Intellectual.' *Society* 47: 430–438.

Williamson, Judith. 1978. *Decoding Advertisements: Ideology and Meaning in Advertising*. London: Marion Boyars.

Open Access This chapter is licensed under the terms of the Creative Commons Attribution 4.0 International License (http://creativecommons.org/licenses/by/4.0/), which permits use, sharing, adaptation, distribution and reproduction in any medium or format, as long as you give appropriate credit to the original author(s) and the source, provide a link to the Creative Commons license and indicate if changes were made.

The images or other third party material in this chapter are included in the chapter's Creative Commons license, unless indicated otherwise in a credit line to the material. If material is not included in the chapter's Creative Commons license and your intended use is not permitted by statutory regulation or exceeds the permitted use, you will need to obtain permission directly from the copyright holder.

CHAPTER 4

Mapping Capital in *Mexico This Month* (1955–1971)

Abstract This chapter, based on original archival work on *Mexico/This Month*, responds to Susannah Glusker's invitation to undertake 'an analysis of [its] contribution … in promoting Mexico' (Glusker 1998: 15), with a particular focus on cartography and capital. The chapter, through a close reading of its trademark Explorers' Maps series, and drawing on pertinent work on cartography from a range of disciplines, suggests that *Mexico This Month* visually and discursively mapped a fantasy of capital that is related to, yet destabilized by, a second, more problematic fantasy of conquest. The chapter also enquires into the impact of capital on the magazine's external periodical code, that is, the relation between the conditions of its state funding and its endurance as a material artifact over its lifetime.

Keywords Art · Commerce · Cartography · Capital · Conquest · Tourism

Maps offer arguments and propositions; they define, recreate, shape and mediate. Invariably, they also fail to reach their objectives. (Brotton 2012: 16)

In a 1959 audit of the travel magazine, *Mexico This Month*, a prospective buyer criticized the quality of its copy, claiming that some of it was 'so badly written that it was impossible to edit'. S/he also censured the inflated wages of its staff artists, indicating that if s/he were to take over the magazine's management, 'I would insist upon firing [them] … and buy such material on an assignment per piece basis'. The North American was exercised by the cost and style of the magazine's artwork, which s/he considered 'pretentious and arty to the extent of being obscure and effete … of a school which I would not, in all justification and knowledge of this business, accept.' In the auditor's view, a magazine for public consumption 'must be on a least common denominator level, communicating instantly the intent of the writer or artist'. The existing artwork, s/he advised, contradicted the commercial aims of the magazine in which 'Good photographic cover would be infinitely better, have more punch and Sell [*sic*] than the obscure approach of [the artist] Vlady who seems dearly in love with his own work'. There was, aside from a practical recommendation to purchase an addressograph, an equally blistering account of the magazine's operations and its 'shameful' mailing and circulation systems: the incumbent editor's laissez faire handling of those affairs was decried as 'a fatal violation of all concepts of publishing' (Brenner 1959). Such unvarnished remarks, without reference to the object of criticism, might lead one to expect little from the periodical in question. In fact, *Mexico This Month* was far from the calamity diagnosed in that withering report. Its seventeen-year run is something of a record in a market 'characterized by a heavy mortality rate', in which other contemporary illustrated magazines in Mexico were vulnerable because of the increasing encroachment of their advertising revenues by television. As Richard D. Woods has observed, in the lifetime of *Mexico This Month* some seven magazines of a similar character, which had an average shelf life of five years, folded (Woods 1990: 209). Moreover, the periodical was well received in the US press as 'fascinating and reasonable' and compared favorably with *The New Yorker* and others of 'our better magazines' (Brenner 1967). Yet the auditor's report is striking as well as strident in its expression of the apparently trenchant dissension between art/culture and commerce, which is one of this book's central concerns. That is, their comments raise issues of a magazine's 'acceptable' content (digesting its defining admixture of visual and written material) and imply a correlation between category or type of magazine and symbolic capital—the popular vs the more high brow publication—in which enduring dichotomy culture is pitted against capital. In what follows, I suggest that such an opposition is not quite as irreducible as that auditor suggests.

This chapter focuses on *Mexico This Month*, a title that was established in Mexico at the height of the country's so-called economic miracle. Based on original archival work on this magazine, which has received no scholarly attention to date, it responds to Susannah Glusker's invitation to undertake 'an analysis of the contribution of *Mexico This Month* in promoting Mexico' (Glusker 1998: 15). First, the chapter elucidates the context of magazine's genesis and gives an account of how *Mexico This Month* operated as a vehicle for boosting tourism and the economy at a critical period of Mexico's modernity. The chapter's second section then attends to the function of what would become in its early years the travel magazine's trademark centrefold maps, which were drawn by the same artist at the receiving end of the auditor's invective cited above. Maps are ubiquitous in the practice and experience of tourism, of course; they convey information about places, provide ideas for journeys, and are also employed by tourists as a means to learn about the histories and environments of different routes and sites.[1] Yet, as Stephen P. Hanna and Vincent J. Del Casino Jr. point out, these material representations of space, 'produced and interpreted in changing social contexts,' are 'complexly and intertextually interrelated with the spaces and identities [they] strive to represent' (2003: xi). Through a close reading of the magazine's Explorers' Maps series, and drawing on pertinent work on cartography from a range of disciplines, I suggest that *Mexico This Month* visually and discursively mapped a fantasy of capital that is related to, yet potentially destabilized by, a second, more complex fantasy of conquest. The third section of the chapter enquires into the impact of capital on the external periodical code of *Mexico This Month*, in particular, the relation of the conditions of the magazine's funding to its existence as a material artefact over its lifetime. The 'mapping' I invoke in the chapter's title, therefore, notwithstanding the term's 'proliferating and metaphorical promiscuity' (Craib 2004: 3), refers to both its literal and symbolic meanings, to the magazine's cartographic content as well as to my methods. Taking my cue from scholars in geography, history, visual culture, and cultural studies who are interested less in 'maps as finished artifacts than ... in mapping as a creative activity' (Corner 1999: 217), the following analysis sheds light on the complex ways in which this magazine was invested in the aesthetics, geopolitics, and economics of tourism during Mexico's post-war/Cold-War years. In essence, it considers the ways in which the Explorers' Maps series of *Mexico This Month* not only represented the country at that time, but imaginatively produced it, for as Jerry Brotton reminds us, 'mapmakers do not just reproduce the world, they construct it' (2012: 7).

I

Mexico This Month first appeared in 1955, in the midst of the decades of rapid economic growth known as the 'Mexican miracle' when, in an indication of the country's newly found economic and political strength, investment in and expansion of the tourism sector increased exponentially. This was a period in which the country was steered towards rampant capitalist development by Miguel Alemán, 'arguably the most important president in twentieth-century Mexican history … [and] a real genius of modern Mexican political life' (Sherman 2010: 537, 538). Alemán's government, dependent on a unique political coalition formed of rich industrialists and a rising urban middle class, accelerated industrialization, invested heavily in infrastructure projects, suppressed trade union activity, and openly courted foreign capital (so much so that 'rich Americans and Mexicans united to a degree not unlike that seen during the *Porfiriato*'). One consequence was indeed an economic 'miracle', in which Mexico averaged close to 6% annual gross domestic product (GDP) growth into the 1960s, 'one of the highest sustained rates recorded in the world' and output from manufacturing, a sector that benefitted especially from the investment of US capital, rose by a factor of ten (Sherman 2010: 544). Another consequence was that, as rural Mexico failed to benefit from the urban development then underway and modernization did nothing to address inequality, *Alemanismo* effectively undid many of the radical reforms put in place by his predecessor Lázaro Cárdenas: as John Sherman puts it, under Alemán, the 'former "enemies" of the Revolution … were now its beneficiaries, and by the time he left office, the "institutionalized revolution" was one only in name' (2010: 539). Thus, the postwar period emblematizes one of the central paradoxes of Mexico's twentieth-century history, which is 'extraordinary in that a revolutionary movement, which experimented with collectivist and even socialist modes of production, led to such a deeply inequitable capitalist regime' (Gillingham and Smith 2014: 2).

Alemán (who was known as 'the father of Mexican tourism') had deeply and personally invested in the development of tourism, from which he amassed a vast personal fortune. On the one hand, as Alex

Saragoza has noted, Alemán made concerted efforts to modernize Mexican tourism: 'Tourists eager to experience "Mexican culture" found an infrastructure to provide it, readymade availability and the exotically different' (2001: 108). On the other hand, Alemán bought and profited from land and property in Baja California and Veracruz as well as prime real estate in Acapulco, which, after the end of his term of presidential office and under his subsequent tenure of the position of Minister of Tourism, became transformed into a world-class resort.[2] Advances in infrastructure facilitated growth in the sector: a number of superhighways were opened in Mexico during the 1950s, including a direct four-lane road south from Mexico City to Acapulco, the transnational Christopher Columbus Pan-American highway from El Paso to the Guatemalan border, and other routes from Nogales to Guadalajara and from Mexico City to Puebla, Cuernavaca, and other cities in the Bajío. By 1957, Mexico had fifteen thousand miles of paved roads, 'a testimony to both the government's commitment to road building and the technology of new paving equipment imported from the United States,' (Sherman 2010: 547) just one indication of the benefit Mexico accrued from US business interests during that period. At the same time there was substantial development and state investment in the aviation industry, to which Acapulco's success owed considerable debt. New routes opened up the skies to a greater number of airlines, while long-standing carrier American Airlines bestowed planes with 'Mexican' names such as 'the Aztec' and 'the Toltec' in order to compete in a more crowded market (Boardman 2001: 95). Further, a new airport opened to the southeast of Acapulco, Guadalajara's airfield was expanded and some $5 million of investment was ploughed into Mexico City's Benito Juarez airport in 1953, which also marked the year of Mexico's first National Tourism Congress (Sherman 2010: 548).

During this Golden Age of prosperity, a self-styled group of businessmen called the Comité norteamericano pro-México launched *Mexico This Month*, under the editorship of Anita Brenner. This group of North American executives, bankers and long-term Mexico City residents formed in June 1954, in the wake of that year's devaluation of the *peso*, with the avowed purpose to 'fomentar las buenas relaciones entre México y los EEUU de Norteamérica, mediante actividades culturales, cívicas y publicitarias' [encourage good relations between Mexico and the United States of North America, through cultural, civic and advertising activities] (Brenner, n.d.). Their congregation, 'set up as a working mechanism to cooperate with the then newly organized National Tourist

Commission, headed by Secretary of the Interior, Angel Carbajal', had official encouragement and endorsement from the Mexican state, the then Finance Minister Gilberto Loyo and President Adolfo Ruiz Cortínez (1:1, 1955, 6). Their endeavours, under the chairmanship of John McIntyre (of General Motors) and the banker William Richardson, were clearly motivated as much by commercial as putatively 'philanthropic' or diplomatic interests, as General Motors and the National City Bank of New York were regular advertisers in the magazine. The magazine was conceived as a means of improving social and business relations between Mexico and the United States by promoting travel, investment, and retirement in Mexico. Brenner articulated her agenda and participation in cultural terms: as a traveller 'who incited travel' (Monsivais 2010: xvii) in journalism and guidebooks throughout her career, she insisted on the need for such a vehicle to project a more progressive image of Mexico to its northern neighbours. The magazine became a tool for counteracting what Brenner described as a prevailing 'desconfianza hacia Mexico' [distrust of Mexico] and a 'prensa hostil' [hostile press] in the north, where Mexico and Latin America had long been viewed as morally decrepit, politically unstable, and economically and racially backward.[3] *Mexico This Month* was thus conceived as a response to a geopolitical as well as an economic crisis. It aimed to intervene in and boost a fitful tourist market in the post-war decades, and, in doing so, promote commercial interests north and south of the border. In this respect it was very much part of what Ricardo Salvatore (1998), drawing on Stephen Greenblatt, terms the representational machines of informal empire, in which business and knowledge are interconnected. *Mexico This Month* announced this purpose in its manifesto, 'Operation Amigos', in the inaugural issue:

> [W]e believe that one of the best ways to create a better understanding between two peoples is through travel. Our main effort is, therefore, being directed to the promotion of increased travel to and from Mexico ... [and] in putting Mexico into English we will be doing our own piece of the big job of rapprochement towards which America is moving ... [for] Today the idea of a thriving and contented neighbor is good business and good politics. (1:1, 1955, 5)

Encouraging tourism and investment was conceived as a means of soft or informal diplomacy, a way of 'hac[iendo] ambiente, para ir desvaneciendo confusiones y agresiones' (Brenner 1964) [creating an atmosphere, in order to dispel misunderstandings or aggressions] or, as Brenner put it elsewhere, 'friendliness, understanding and helpfulness as a good international recipe' (*MTM*, 2:4, 1956, 7).[4] In an industry in which 'even the slightest hint of danger can destroy a destination' (Clancy 2001: 127), and in the context of a country sensitive to criticism abroad, as we saw in the Introduction, the potential impact of the magazine's efforts to counter adverse images of Mexico, to 'bring dollars down, to help ease away unnecessary or unreal fears' (Brenner 1955), cannot be underestimated.

But how did the magazine do this exactly? From its inception, *Mexico This Month* was conceived as a bi-national project, as 'la voz de Mexico en inglés' [the voice of Mexico in English] (Brenner, n.d.). It brought together unknown and established Mexican and North American writers and artists to promote the country's history, geography and culture, some of the better known of which were Frank Brandenburg, Leonora Carrington, Matias Goeritz, Juan Rulfo, and Leopoldo Zea. Brenner's insistence on their 'non-professional' status as writers and artists, rather than journalists and illustrators ('we knew nothing about business, production, advertising or distribution' she claims, 2:4, 1956, 7) was strategic. On one level, as Faye Hammill and Michelle Smith suggest, invoking 'originality and artistry rather than technique and craftsmanship, indicate[s] an aspiration towards high culture which is typical of the middlebrow [magazine]' (2015: 87). On another level, however, in the case of *Mexico This Month*, it underscores the avowed function of the magazine's collective 'unbusiness-like objectives' (14:4, 1958, 7) as cultural and diplomatic (rather than wholly commercial) work, while potentially forestalling the kind of wounding public criticism Brenner encountered earlier in her career, in the *Holiday* debacle discussed in the Introduction. In its early years, the magazine's international roster of contributors was a badge of honour ('on our staff are represented six nationalities, about double the number of languages ... about the only other place a staff like this could be found in one enterprise might be Paris'). This speaks not only to the large influx of foreigners visiting and residing in Mexico since the 1920s and 1930s, but also to the magazine's tactical cosmopolitanism; that is, 'the dynamics of good-neighbour ideas at work ... a sort of pilot project of the nations in the hopeful building of a saner world' (3:4, 1957, 7). A letter from the US ambassador Fulton Freeman thanking Brenner for her efforts at 'correcting some misleading impressions about Mexico and its relations with the US' published in the magazine endorsed and legitimized these endeavours: 'Real success [in promoting understanding between peoples],' Freeman wrote, 'depends upon the kind of initiative and sense of responsibility shown by private citizens like yourself and *Mexico This Month*' (X:11, 1965, 8).

In essence, in its focus on sites of touristic interest, aspects of Mexico's cultural heritage, indigenous peoples and traditions, as well as its social and political life, *Mexico This Month* was a blend of the kind of coverage offered by its bilingual predecessor *Mexican Folkways* and its counterpart *Mexican Life*, with the more popular tone and look of magazines on both sides of the border such as *Life* and *Siempre!* Those, as part of their 'modern' agenda, attempted to engage readers by placing a strong emphasis on visuality and by covering the lives of celebrities. Thus, *Mexico This Month* ran special issues on different regions of the country, highlighting places of touristic interest. It combined features on destinations such as the capital, the Colonial Cities and Acapulco; on museums, archaeological sites and fiestas, together with seasonal advice for travellers on what to pack and what to wear, a series on 'Basic Mexican', as well as coverage of, say, 'The Kennedy Sensation' on JFK's 1962 visit to the country. Like *Mexican Folkways*, *Mexico This Month* also covered and promoted the work of Mexican artists, *inter alia* Diego Rivera, José Clemente Orozco, Leonora Carrington and Francisco Goitia, a profile of whom in the magazine's second issue was illustrated with photographs by Edward Weston. Writers were also featured: *Mexico This Month* commemorated the award of the 1958 Villarutia prize to Octavio Paz for his *El arco y la lira*, for example, and covered the furore provoked by the publication by the Fondo de cultura económica of Oscar Lewis's *The Children of Sanchez*, a work of an 'outsider' speaking of the squalor that afflicted large parts of Mexico.[5] Like Toor with *Mexican Folkways*, Brenner envisioned a pedagogical and archival function to *Mexico This Month*: in a reformulated manifesto-cum-advertisement in the magazine's January 1968 issue, she maintained that 'it is regularly used as reference by key people in politics, publishing, business and education throughout the US' and 'is the only English language publication on Mexico used regularly and widely for reference and study in US schools' (XIII:1, 1968, 1).

Encouragement of tourism and investment took variegated forms in *Mexico This Month*. More overtly, these included a regular column called 'National Panorama', which reported to readers on the stock market situation; on the country's banking laws; on aspects of government policy (recounting a presidential address, for example, or a piece—written by Loyo—on foreign investment in Mexico). The overwhelming emphasis in such items was on the country's political stability, its economic security, and the benefits of development and industrialization. Richardson writes in the magazine's debut issue of 'a combination of conditions [that] makes Mexico one of the best risks available to capital in Latin America' (1:1, 1955, 4), for instance; while the regular News and Comment section documented 'the increased confidence and security of the Mexican economy' (1:4, 1955), some issues later 'placing Mexico definitely in the industrial age and as a modern nation' (2:4, 1956, 8). Throughout its lifetime, the magazine published features by leading figures in the tourism industry, such as Gustavo Ortiz Hernán, director of the Mexican government Tourist Bureau, and it published special numbers in May 1958 on 'Tourism' and in November 1970 on 'Convention Mexico', the latter in collaboration with the National Tourism Council, the Mexico City Convention Center and the state Tourism Department. The inclusion of a pull-out 'Happy shoppers' map of where to spend money in Mexico City effectively' (2:12, December 1956), as well as a special series on retirement (entitled 'Search for Eden') and regular articles on the purchase of property were other iterations of that same agenda.[6] In 'The Real Estate Story', for example, readers were urged to

> Go out and buy yourself a house ... you'll have a wonderful time with it ... be sure not to feel the curbs of convention ... The Mexican way is strictly freedom to style your own. (4:10, 1958, 23)

Meanwhile, in a piece called 'Taxco suitcase', 'wise visitors' were advised 'to leave at least half their suitcase vacant for silver, its innumerable varieties of jewelry, flatware and so on' (2:6, 1956, 5). Moreover, the magazine ran abundant advertising from major companies such as General Electric, Ford, Mobiloil, Air France, Aerolíneas Mexicanas, Monsanto, Bacardi, Chanel, and Nescafé. Some of this copy was tactically 'indigenized', a marketing manoeuvre then in vogue, as we saw earlier with American Airlines; for example, General Motors affiliated the ancient engineering feats of the Aztecs to the complex technology of its Buick model, depicting in a hand-drawn illustration the pyramids at Teotihuacán in an advertisement in the December 1956 issue.

In essence, through all of these means, Mexico was imagined as a large potential market, a magnet for consumers and investors alike. It is notable that during a decade in which the country was developing a reputation as a haven for alterity and adventure for bohemian visitors from the North, the longer-stay visitors of *Mexico This Month*'s readership—an older, affluent demographic of professionals and businessmen—were of particular interest to the Mexican state. For while the 'miracle' had been successful in augmenting their number, the type of US tourist attracted to Mexico had also by the mid 1950s begun to cause concern, as Michael Clancy has observed: 'Short stays contributed to relatively low spending per visit and the reputation of border areas as centres of vice and smuggling intensified' (2001: 45).

More subtle devices in the magazine to foster a sense of hemispheric fraternity and intimacy, and to convey this shift in Mexico's reputation from that of the unruly to the good neighbour, included a regular page of readers' correspondence. This was a forum that functioned much like an information bureau in print form and which eventually became known as 'The Question Desk'. It addressed queries from 'Monthers' (as the magazine fondly addressed its readers) regarding accommodation, routes, or shipping charges and facilitated the purchase of particular consumer items: notwithstanding the kind of postal inefficiencies discussed in Chapter 1, this was eventually formalized into a paid-for service.[7] Also published was readers' correspondence on issues germane to the periodical. 'I found the magazine real chatty—like a nice intimate conversation—or a letter from home' (6:4, April 1960, 6), observed one; another urged the editor, '*por favor*, don't ever make *Mexico This Month* too slick, too proofread. Love it the way it is' (10:9, 1965, 28); while another, a high school principal from New York, complained about the content not being appropriate for his eight-year-old pupils, 'you will recall that we told you all about tequila and things' (8:7, October 1962). Yet readers also responded to and enquired about the particularities of the country's politics and culture: 'Can you please tell us how Mexico operates as a democracy with apparently only one political party?' (6:4, April 1960, 6).

In an editorial entitled 'Person to Person', Brenner addressed readers directly in every issue, focusing on an item of topical interest, or interpreting an aspect of Mexico's culture or current events. At times the editorial provided a space in which she defended Mexico's efforts in international relations, especially in light of disadvantageous coverage north of the border with/in the United States. In this respect, and in the broader context of the Cold War, when international tourism became codified symbolically and politically as a democratic activity, the magazine operated explicitly as a form of informal international diplomacy. This is a testament to the power of mainstream consumer publications to 'produce publics and counterpublics' and 'advance particular causes' (Hammill et al. 2015: 12). In an August 1955 issue, for example, Brenner decried the 'horrendous picture of this country on the skids' painted by [North] American journalism, lamenting that the only beneficiary of such enmity between neighbours could be 'the Moscow mill' (1:3, 1955, 7). Elsewhere, in relation to that same climate of heightened suspicion and distrust, Brenner was forced to clarify and distinguish the magazine's use of the word communal from 'that other word' (1:7, 1955, 7). Consistently, through this channel, Brenner drew her readers' attention to Mexico's geopolitical strength and its potential for leadership within Latin America more generally, insisting that 'what's good for Mexico, is likely to be good for the US' (6:4, 1960, 7): 'she alone possesses the material basis for continental leadership … no Latin country is better equipped to interpret Latin America to the US' (5:4, 1959, 23). More controversially for her US readers, from 1960 onwards Brenner used the 'Person to Person' editorial to defend Mexico's stance on Cuba, which rested on a policy of non-intervention (though opposed to Soviet militarization, Mexico was supportive of Castro's revolutionary social and economic reforms):

> It is the impression of the Cubans that the American government is trying to bully them, and this is also to a considerable extent the impression in Mexico and other Latin American countries. Having been indubitably bullied themselves, Mexicans often hair-trigger to any merest hint of a suggestion of this, so, though they may be looking askance at Castro as you are, they figure it's up to the *Cubans* who they want at the head of their government. (6:8, 1960, 7, original emphasis)

This editorial was followed by a feature by Daniel James in the October 1960 edition called 'Mexico is Mexico' in which he assured that, while unprepared to condemn Castro, Mexico remained opposed to communism—'Mexico is not going to imitate Cuba' (8)—and that the maintenance of the friendliest possible relations with the US was a cornerstone of Mexican policy. Notwithstanding, over subsequent months and years the letters pages of *Mexico This Month*, attested to the polarised responses to that position and of the magazine's alignment with it: on the one hand, indignation at the periodical's 'ultra-liberal' attitude (7:1, 1961, 28) and cancelled subscriptions ('I intend to have nothing to do with Mexico or things Mexican in the future', 6:10, 1960, 6) and, on the other, unqualified support, urging the reprinting of the magazine's editorial material on the matter in all major US newspapers. Brenner vindicated the stance in her coverage of President López Mateos's 1963 European tour and his policies on nuclear disarmament, claiming that: 'Mexico's positions of being neither "neutral" nor even "uncommitted" exactly, but just plain not belligerent, however cold the war' afforded it 'a torch-bearing role' in peace work (9:2, 1963, 10). At all times, and whatever the subject, Brenner sought to reconcile her writing in that and other sections of the magazine with its congenial politics: 'The style,' she avowed, 'has been kept easy and casual on the theory that a tone as of an acquaintance or friend talking is better than noise and bombast' (Brenner 1964).[8]

II

One of the most striking aspects of *Mexico This Month*'s visual repertoire in its early years was a series of hand-drawn, centrefold maps of Mexico, its capital and other popular tourist destinations such as Veracruz and Acapulco. Created by its staff artist, Vladimir Machados (the *nom de plume* of a Russian émigré artist then resident in the capital and son of the exiled revolutionary novelist Victor Serge), these colourful 'Explorers' Maps' distilled various facets of the prevailing tourist discourse about Mexico as an embodiment of modernity and antiquity. The series was published at a time when there were significant advances made in the production of tourism maps. Although the coupling of maps and tourism dates back to the late nineteenth century, when large oil companies spotted the promotional potential for marketing their products and printed road maps to be given away for free at petrol stations, the close association between the two became consolidated particularly during the interwar period.[9] Technological developments and diminishing production costs meant that maps had become cheaper to produce and tourism maps, 'creat[ing] an idealized image of their chosen location so that it would appeal more powerfully to their customer', became more affordable and more widely distributed than ever before. Indeed, it was precisely in the 1950s when such maps also started to become more elaborate, embellished with colourful images and notes about interesting places to stop en route. As Tom Harper has observed: 'Maps in guidebooks and postcards illustrated commercial air travel routes and holiday destinations, using colour, advertisement, and a highly pictorial style to enhance their appeal' (2016: 169). Accordingly, the Explorers' Maps series of *Mexico This Month*—which included an array of plans of cities, states, highways, ports, and fishing zones—in addition to promoting the country's security and stability, emphasized Mexico's accessibility and navigability. To some degree, the maps served like conventional tourism maps or those in a travel or guidebook: to provide a chart of a particular destination, say, or a bird's-eye view of the nation's geography, as well as to orient and enable readers to traverse routes to, in, and between different locations. Yet, rather than mere visual adjuncts or simple guides to the routes travelled, the series' maps constitute complex representations with their own narrative and iconographic qualities and histories. Indeed, the story of the Explorers' Map series of *Mexico This Month* that unfolds here is one about maps as intertextual objects which, as Hanna and del Casino argue in their work on the 'map space', 'are materially interconnected to other spaces and texts, both past and present, and are thus rich sites for the critical interrogation of tourism practices and spaces' (Hanna and del Casino 2003: xxvi). In contrast to the 'pseudo-objectivity' of plain 'scientific' maps, the *Mexico This Month* centrefolds were highly stylized and embellished pictorial maps that often belied the avowed (but now increasingly disputed) clarity and neutrality of cartographic technology. Further, as will become clear in what follows, the Explorers' Maps visualized and affirmed Mexico's diversity and history in complex, even contradictory ways.

Maps have long been bound up in the articulation of power and authority, the geographical information they relay typically the preserve of ruling elites: as such, throughout history, as Jerry Brotton observes, 'for shamans, savants, rulers and religious leaders, maps … [have] conferred arcane, magical authority on their makers and owners' (2012: 3). This has a particular resonance in the context under scrutiny here, where, since Independence, as an emerging nation Mexico has been subject to repeated journeys of mapping, 'the means by which to identify and assume control over resources, to reconfigure property relations, and to generate knowledge of the territory' as well as to document customs and character. Indeed, mapping became such an obsession of agrarian bureaucrats and state officials in modern Mexico, that, Raymond

Craib avows, 'one could plausibly argue that the state and cartography are reciprocally constitutive' (Craib 2004: 9). Yet that enterprise to create a spatial imaginary of Mexico (a 'state fixation', as Craib puts it) was not uncomplicated but a 'much more ambivalent and dialectical process than one of some state juggernaut imposing its visions upon an either quiescent or intransigent countryside' (Craib 2004: 13). The readings of the Explorers' Maps of *Mexico This Month* that follow attest to that very complexity. However, if framing is a territorializing gesture, as Denis Cosgrove (1999) reminds us, the magazine centrefolds' repeated emphasis on visualizing Mexico as a discrete political unit, in addition to establishing a discursive intertextuality within and beyond the series, speaks to an issue of 'branding'—as much of the periodical as of the nation itself—and insinuates a nationalist rhetoric of sorts.[10] That is, the visual recurrence of and insistence on Mexico's human, cultural, and political geography over the four years of the Explorers' Map series' existence (the whole sequence of images comprising an atlas in serialised form) resonates with efforts at a national level during that period to assert the country's identity as a modern Republic, to enable readers within and outside the country to recognize and identify (with) Mexico and to provide a sense of belonging to a nation. For, as Ricardo Padrón observes, 'the form of collective self-fashioning that we know as the nation-state ... is inseparable from a clear image of a territory that inspires our affection, demands our loyalty, calls us home' (2004: 9).

The iconic power of the nation's contours was not lost on advertisers in the pages of *Mexico This Month*. Kodak, in one of its advertisements in the magazine, used an image of a reel of camera film shaped in the recognizable form of Mexico's geography, in order to assure readers that 'It's the same word in Mexico!'.[11] Kodak's appropriation of Mexico's semblance to a cornucopia is pertinent: it recalls another key function of maps, to 'support capitalism both practically and ideologically' (Harper 2016: 141), not only as commodities in themselves, but in their very production as a profit-making enterprise.[12] The commercial importance of maps dates back to the colonial period under the Portuguese and Spanish empires, which established their value as route-finding tools and tried to standardize their production by means of institutions like the Casa de la Contratación (House of Trade) in Seville.[13] Yet, the then reduced publishing industry in the Iberian peninsula compared to that of northern Europe lead to a significant paradox: that is, as Brotton describes, that 'the maps they produced were invariably hand-drawn in a futile attempt to limit their circulation' at a time when 'a new world was being defined by new ways of making money' (Brotton 2012: 263, 264). *Mexico This Month* provided symbolic and concrete means for its readers of satisfying that same acquisitive impulse in the modern period. For instance, the recurrence of an imperial figure in the Explorers' Maps series—whether invoked in narrative or in pictorial form (as was also the case in the images accompanying the 'Search for Eden' series on retirement, which commonly included the figure of a Spanish conquistador bearing golf clubs)—speaks to commercial activity and infers that modern Mexico was still ripe for exploration, exploitation, and extraction. In the twentieth-century age of mechanical reproduction, a further (historical) contradiction emerges in relation to these images of the Explorers' Maps, which were distributed separately from their original form in the series precisely because of their hand-drawn, 'Colonial' style. Following their widespread appeal and success, the Explorers' Maps were marketed and sold individually as artisanal, 'folkloric' products. This pull-out, spin-off function speaks to the map's potential as commodity, as mentioned above, and also to the broader operations of modern capitalism in which the magazine was invested and which it sought to foster. Although in this instance the maps were sold in portable foldaway leaflets, in some cases it is debatable how much practical use they would have been for orientation purposes (a point to which I return below): indeed, it is praise for their aesthetic or souvenir value as artefacts that is documented in the readers' and editorial pages of the magazine. Nevertheless, in both centrefold and separate leaflet forms, the maps were bound up in a long tradition of mapping for commercial purposes as well as in the magazine's early attempts at diversification, name recognition, and loyalty. If the hand-drawn was invoked in the colonial period as a means to curtail, it was now deployed as a technology from which to expand circulation.

Insofar as the Explorers' Maps of *Mexico This Month* were about identity, collectability, and ersatz utility, they spoke an equivocal visual language, fusing the geographical with the thematic, the narrative with the iconographic, devices modern with pre-modern. That fusion of seemingly dialectical characteristics is inherent in the design and construction of maps themselves: as 'graphic representations that facilitate a spatial understanding of things, concepts, conditions, processes, or events in the human world' (Harley and Woodward 1992: xvi), all maps are always already hybrid, variegated texts in form and composition. Throughout history they have appeared in myriad material forms, including cloth, tablet, drawing, and print, and while they exist as material objects maps are graphic documents that are at once written and visual: as Brotton remarks, 'you cannot understand a map without writing, but a map without a visual element is simply a collection of place names' (2012: 5). Likewise, insofar as all maps are to some degree shaped by scientific principles or data, 'there has always been art in cartography' (Harmon 2009: 9). That is, not only are artistic skills and techniques required in order to make 'an ultimately imaginative representation of an unknowable object (the world)' and produce an abstraction of it to 'a series of geometrical lines and shapes' but they can also be applied creatively to enhance a map's effect. Indeed, it was in the last decades of the twentieth century, following the decolonization of many developing countries and during the greater economic and political uncertainties of the 1960s and 1970s, that there was an 'exponential increase in artists [themselves] working with maps' (Harmon 2009: 9). Gayle Clemans usefully sums up the differences in cartographic practice: if geographers 'submit to a tacit agreement to obey certain mapping conventions, to speak in a malleable but standardized visual language. Artists are free to disobey these rules' (Harmon 2009: 10).

The Explorers' Maps series was no exception in this respect, its creator(s) proving to be incisive and creative in their insertion into this aesthetic and political legacy. For example, the magazine archly claims its map of La Lagunilla in Mexico City (a traditional market held over several blocks of the city centre, where 'quite literally anything can be bought') to be 'so far as we know, the first effort ever made at a truly scientific survey of this fascinating territory' (1:9, 1955, 13) (Fig. 4.1).

Fig. 4.1 Explorer's map of La Lagunilla market, *Mexico This Month*, 1:9, 1955

Continuing on this theme, the map's legend declares that it shows 'the exact location of each speciality and direction of traffic', with each subset of merchandise sold at the market indicated by blue and white pictorial figures located at particular junctures on a grid formation of streets. Major thoroughfares are identified by name (República de Honduras, República del Perú, and so on), as are some buildings by their commercial use. The faux cartographic precision of this discernibly hand-drawn plan is both enhanced and offset by its decorative colours: the market's domain is defined by an area in an arresting shade of deep pink, the borders beyond which are in a majestic purple. This vivid drawing, 'done in Colonial style, printed in three [*sic*] colours on fine paper, ready for framing or guiding explorers' (1:9, 1955, 28) became the prototype for the magazine's series of portable maps for purchase.

In the Explorers' Maps of the Paseo de la Reforma and Chapultepec, which portray one of Mexico City's main avenues and parks respectively, key buildings, sites, and monuments—such as Bellas Artes, the Torre Latinoamericana, and the Angel of Independence—are highlighted on the itineraries through vast distortions in perspective as well as through their depictions in the kind of intense colours that emblazoned the Lagunilla map, in these cases red and white against a black filler and green background in the former, blue, grey, and white in the latter. As a result, in terms of the absence of any information pertaining to scale or projection as well as their embellishments in proportion and colour, both maps have the look of caricature, in which respect they are likely to have had touristic appeal as the collectable items they became after publication.

The Reforma map (Fig. 4.2), which appeared in the September 1958 issue, and was co-produced by Machados and C. van Millingen, conveys a strong sense of the capital city's architectural hybridity, as it plots a visual itinerary of one of Mexico City's most important arteries and a history of downtown establishments and sites of interest. These are documented in two separate but consecutive legends in the upper left-hand and lower right-hand corners of the map. The Paseo de la Reforma was originally opened in the 1860s under Emperor Maximilian as a way to link the Castillo de Chapultepec in the west of the city with the central main square, the Zócalo. As such, it is an avenue of considerable historical as well as geographical importance in Mexico City, consisting of a wide central thoroughfare bisecting once elegant neighbourhoods populated by the Porfirian gentry and flanked on either side by a double row of trees, private mansions, and apartment buildings that began to appear

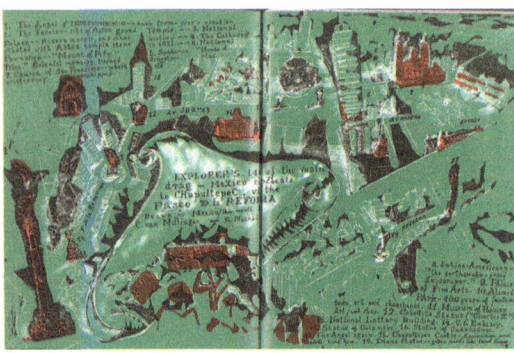

Fig. 4.2 Explorer's map of the main drag in Mexico city, via the Paseo de la Reforma, *Mexico This Month*, 4:9, 1958

in the 1890s.[14] The 'spine of the ideal city', as Mauricio Tenorio Trillo puts it, the Paseo de la Reforma was developed during the *Porfiriato* as a chronological reconstruction of the nation's history, one 'that aimed to reconcile the ideas and events of a real past with the ideals and needs of an inexperienced ruling class that was trying to guide a new nation' (Johns 1997: 24). The form that took along this boulevard was the erection of a series of monuments of national heroes including Charles IV, Columbus, and Cuauhtémoc, which, together with the Angel of Independence are positioned in an arrangement that 'all but ignored Mexico's past as a colony while praising the European world that Spain had introduced it to' and 'celebrated Mexico's roots in Aztec society, but uncertainly' (Johns 1997: 24), as Michael Johns remarks.[15]

On the *Mexico This Month* map, at either end of the route, there is the Zócalo ('site of Aztec grand temple' the legend tells us) and Chapultepec Castle ('Maximilian and Carlota lived there') while along it are depicted Sanborns ('Colonial mansion turned drugstore plus'), the Torre Latinoamericana ('the earthquake-proof skyscraper') and the Alameda Park ('400 years of fountains, books, art and shoeshines'). The Angel of Independence, in the map's lower left-hand corner and the Zócalo, in the top right-hand corner, frame the route spatially and aesthetically: as with the Cathedral, Chapultepec Castle, the Museum of Popular Art, and the statues to Charles IV ('el Caballito'), Columbus, and Cuauhtémoc along the Reforma, the red and black shading of white line drawings highlight and animate those buildings and statues in expressive fashion. The map's intense colours are evocatively cast in the hues of the Mexican national flag, predominant in the maps' green background, white line drawings, and red shading. The dominance in the lower left-hand corner of the map of the Angel monument, 'conceived as the universal symbol of Mexico's modernism and sovereignty', underscores that chromatic allusion to nationalism, for as Tenorio writes, 'El Angel is the nation, apparently accepted by all, though revered in different ways' (2012: 22, 24). Moreover, the map's urban landscape is dominated by the height of its soaring skyscrapers, its towering Torre, and other prominent monuments that surge from ground level (as well as from the constrictions of the 'normative' urban grid) at random, oblique angles and jostle for the readers' eyes and attention. For all that riotous spectacle, however, this is a city plan haunted by vacancy; the unfilled outlines of unpopulated buildings, anonymous apartment blocks, and avenues empty of pedestrian and vehicular traffic. As such, the dynamic but unoccupied Paseo de la Reforma map speaks of the city's aspirations and reach: it functions both as an assertion of the country's historical achievements and contemporary ambitions *and* as an invitation, one that promises to the city's visitors availability, potentiality, and wonder.

The Map of Chapultepec Woods, which appeared in the magazine in January 1956, works with a more orthodox sense of proportion, save, once again, for the depiction of the Angel monument that looms large in the map's top right-hand corner (Fig. 4.3). In contrast to the emptied built environment of the Reforma image, this cartographic close-up of a 'forest park with a castle on a hill' ('the most romantic spot in fabled and storied Mexico City', 2:1, 1956, 13), now home to the official

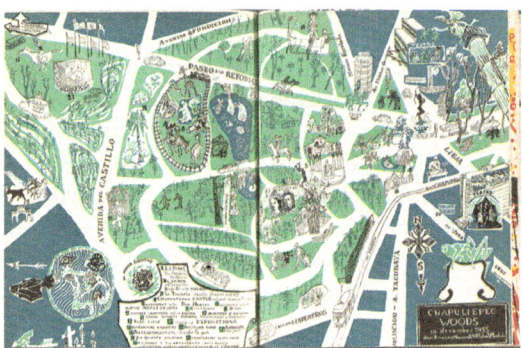

Fig. 4.3 Map of Chapultepec Woods, *Mexico This Month*, 2:1, 1956

presidential residence, is teeming with pictorial figures, bustling activity and movement, of people, animals, and various modes of transit (car, bus, tram, and horse). The bucolic quality of the park, its zoo and planting (its thousands of distinctive *ahuehuete* trees)—'[with] the air of a place in which Druids are still very much at home and where anything can happen' (2:1, 1956, 13)—is emphasized by the soft green colouring of the map's black, green, and white palette and contrasts with the urban pleasures and entertainments (restaurant, cinema, and theatres) situated at its gates. The whole map is about sports and leisure pursuits available at this site—whether football, horse-riding, driving, tennis, bullfighting or boating, alongside eating and attending the theatre or cinema—multiple pastimes for a retreat for Mexico City dwellers and visitors alike. Like all good tourism maps, the Chapultepec plan provides navigable pathways and routes, shaded white, throughout this animated and verdant site. The singular qualities of this space as respite from Mexico City's quotidian geography and temporality are enhanced by the lack of detail provided of the spaces surrounding the park, except for a collection of named avenues such as Reforma and Avenida del Castillo, which are devoid of physical detail and whose dark turquoise fillers give the impression of their submergence under water, a visual reminder perhaps of the springs lying below Chapultepec that once supplied the city's drinking water (Brenner 1932: 108).

The quality of excess evinced in both maps of the Reforma and Chapultepec—which is at stake in many others of the Explorers' Maps series, in different ways—is significant in these cases also at a phenomenological level. As Rob Shields avers, tourism maps have an especially close relationship to bodily experience: they provide sources of guidance for those unfamiliar with the place 'to fit into a ritualized path … eliminating the necessity of asking directions from locals' (2003: 16). Indeed, as a form, the map conventionally rests on notions of containment and accessibility, on encouraging the traversal of space with ease. The proportional and aesthetic distortions in the Paseo de la Reforma map, however, emphasize density, verticality, and depth, and necessarily move the tourist gaze away from ground level to attend to the circuitous and vertiginous negotiation of the route/site and the historical character of urban space. Shields' observations on the function of maps as props are particularly resonant here in respect of both the Reforma and Chapultepec maps: 'representing an entire city or a day's walk in a map, [tourism maps] distance the tourist, nose in map, from the everyday interaction of residents,' he writes. The Explorers' Maps' coverage, design, and their characteristic colourings also direct the experiential and embodied quality of the visit, 'making the tourist *present* in a specific, tinted ... staging of place' (Shields 2003: 16).

If the time-honoured accessibility promised by cartography is undermined by the subjectivity of the Explorers' Maps (which also calls into question their utility as material objects), the expression and promotion of Mexico's modernity in *Mexico This Month*, to which I referred in the previous section, is in turn destabilized by the map series' particular aesthetic. In terms of composition, the maps repeatedly deploy cartouches, alongside other cartographic signs and symbols that evoke the iconographic language of colonial, and pre-modern, map making. In this regard, the imperial figure featured in the Search for Eden series mentioned above recalls the tour describers of early maps, which indicated the military and commercial operations that made possible the fabrication of a geographical plan at all (its sporting guise as a golfer in *Mexico This Month* alluding to the imperialist underpinnings of modern leisure travel) (de Certeau 1984: 121) (Fig. 4.4).

This figure also appears in 'The Trail of Cortés: A Map for Intrepid Explorers' (3:8, August, 1957), which invites readers to re-trace the original colonial incursion from Veracruz to Tenochtitlán, through various key battle sites. The image's asymmetry in scale between the large pictorial figure of an armoured Spanish conquistador and other symbols which dominate the route and the minute, indecipherable urban plans of Veracruz and Tenochtitlán that frame the beginning and end of the trail is telling. Although the legend names eleven stages along the way, including Jalapa, Tlaxcala, and Cholula, otherwise the urban plans are unreadable. 'The Trail of Cortés' map is not so much about how to negotiate

Fig. 4.4 Trail of Cortés, a map for intrepid explorers, *Mexico This Month*, 3:8, 1957

that route, therefore, than about the history that has shaped it. The map's symbols and figures—including a pre-Columbian temple, a serpent, a collection of skulls, and other pictorial figures depicting, at different junctures, Cortez and La Malinche, Spanish conquistadors on horseback or in battle—tell that story in iconographic form. In this respect, while obviously concerned with the representation of space, as Brotton avers and as this image evinces, maps are also often about time, 'ask[ing] viewers to observe how ... events unfold one after another' (Brotton 2012: 5).

Likewise, the 'Wayward Wanderers' Map of Oaxaca' ('an enchanting state, with lovely ladies, handsome dishes, and fine old ruins') plots a human geography of rich and varied ethnicity and history (Fig. 4.5). Here, the southern state's diverse indigenous inhabitants (including the Tejuana and the Mixteca) populate a landscape inhabited by fourteen human figures all dressed in traditional clothing (a key to which is also provided, 'for those who wish to go native', as the map's legend puts it). Each of the figures is devoid of facial features and identified only by means of their distinctive 'costumes', one implication of which is that they are seen as 'types', rather than individuals, whose identities are easily assimilable. That nine of the fourteen figures are 'lovely ladies' indicates too how 'gender is bound up with the nation' (Radcliffe 2011: 209). Such a map has precedents in nineteenth-century imagery of Mexicans as types, as in publications such as *Trajes Mexicanos* by Casimiro Castro and J. Campillo, which was part of a broader nationalist endeavour after Independence to generate images of the land and people to form and disseminate the idea of nation for internal and external consumption. As such, as Magalí Carrera points out, there is an element of *bricolage* in all maps, which may be understood as 'assemblages, collages, and

Fig. 4.5 Wayward Wanderers' map of Oaxaca, *Mexico This Month*, 3:10, 1957

montages of fragments of earlier maps; debris from previous misrepresentations of spaces and shards of current and past visual images' (2011: 8). The 'Wayward Wanderers' Map of Oaxaca' visually articulates the construction of the map as palimpsest. By way of contrast to the vivid colours of the Indians' clothing, a black and white sketch of Monte Albán in an insert in the map's top right-hand corner provides a ground-level view of those 'fine old ruins': hand-written lettering on the illustration indicates that they are where the 'great Zapotec past is discovered'. Together, the bird's eye view of the state's Indian peoples and the 'close-up' perspectives constitute 'unrealizable views and impossible landscapes in which geographically disparate features [are] collapsed into, and actively ordered within, a single frame' (Craib 2011: 154). While the reader is ostensibly invited to survey Oaxaca 'from an elevated ... Apollonian position', in this map there is in fact little prospect of 'light[ing] out across the territory, for there [is] no "space" in which to wander' (Padrón 2004: 60, 61). In spite of the patent ethnic diversity illustrated therein, the region's physical geography is largely bare and the human geography frozen in space and time. Notwithstanding the pictorial image of a train and the railway lines that bisect the state, the map underscores the region's separatist and anachronistic identity: contained and constrained by a thick, bold, red and white border beyond which the roads and train lines featured on the map do not extend, and the space beyond which is blank, Oaxaca is depicted as a place outside of modernity, outside the nation even. Moreover, its ancient peoples are kept ancient, bound ineluctably to the ruins of a pre-Columbian site: they too are both within and outside the nation/history. On some level, of course, as much as it illustrates and instructs less-informed readers about the state's and country's differences, such an image is clearly also invested in the longstanding appeal to Mexico's ethnic diversity as a (re)source to be exploited and/or appropriated. In addition to 'the fantasy of capital' sustained in the magazine by the various means described in the previous section, to some degree, the Oaxaca and 'The Trail of Cortez' maps also perpetuate the ongoing fantasy of conquest promised by travel to Mexico.[16] Indeed, they speak precisely to the ways in which 'maps validate the existence of economic productivity [and colonial extraction] by illustrating it' (Harper 2016: 169).

One of the most vivid representations of the country in these terms and as 'an anachronistic space' (McClintock 1995: 40) is perhaps the 'Complete Explorers' Map for Treasure Hunters on Land and Sea' (Fig. 4.6), which envisages the booty available at various sites across Mexico and its surrounding fishing waters. Here, the fantasy of capital

Fig. 4.6 The Complete Explorers' map for Treasure Hunters on Land and Sea, *Mexico This Month*, 3:11, 1957

and the fantasy of conquest coalesce. As with 'The Trail of Cortés', the 'Treasure Hunters' map depicts a land haunted by its colonial history: the only figures populating the landmass are the 'Guardian ghosts' cheekily peeking out from behind the blocks of explanatory text that appear at different locations, the surrounding blank spaces of the rest of the territory enunciating what Simon Ryan calls 'a statement of economic and demographic availability' (Ryan 1994: 126–127). Indeed, that in this aqueous image the country seems to be almost entirely submerged (nestled in the yellowing sea bed) would seem to reinforce at least one of the terms of that persistent myth of Mexico as a 'dark-skinned Atlantis' (Tenorio Trillo 2010: 20). The explanatory text of the map's narrative labels, however, is marked by a fundamental belatedness, a 'post-touristic irony' evident in other parts of the magazine at different junctures: one label indicates the lost city of Tapoya ('But some people have been here'); another at Los Frailes Mine documents 'the secret of this treasure was kept to avoid paying taxes. You know how it is'; while yet another, at one of Mexico's most visited pre-Columbian archeological sites, reads 'Tomb 7 at Monte Albán – sorry you've been beaten to it'. In this regard, rather than constitute what Michel de Certeau balefully calls 'procedures for forgetting' (1984: 97), the maps of *Mexico This Month*—while insisting, to be sure, on Mexico's continuing potential as a colonial frontier—also underscore the centrality of history and memory to the journey experience there. In this respect, they function in similar terms to the maps that Owen Dwyer, drawing elsewhere on the work of Pierre Nora, calls memorial texts, 'in which the basis for a particular interpretation is endlessly deferred to other texts' with the result being 'the mutual constitution of text and context' (Dwyer 2003: 33). In logging the original and subsequent forms of conquest and exploitation in this manner, the Explorers' Maps interpellate the 'post-tourist' who 'knows that tourism is a series of games with multiple texts and no single, authentic experience' (Urry 2002: 91). In doing so, they also point to a playful revival of the 'pre-modern' function of the map as history book. To some extent this gesture might be seen as part of a larger shift in map production in the late twentieth century mentioned earlier, one which anticipates the emergence of more resistant kinds of cartography (in the form of anti-capitalist maps, for example) from the 1960s onwards. In any case, the Explorers' Maps articulate a complex epistemology regarding the very travel experience and industry in which *Mexico This Month* was invested and which it promoted. In a manner akin to germane Situationist projects, the series invokes but at the same time wrests mapping from 'the colonizing agency of survey and control' to destabilize its own authoritarian and territorializing origins. As such, it crystallizes that central paradox identified by Craib in his excellent study of cartography in Mexico. That is, the maps of *Mexico This Month* visualize a tension between the desired fixation of space (in the very drawing up of the map) and what Craib calls the 'fugitive' quality of the landscape, 'places created and recreated through the prism of memory [...] rather than through the lens of instrumentation' (Craib 2004: 12).[17]

Maps, as Jeremy Black claims and as we have seen from the examples discussed here, are similar to caricatures. The Explorers' Maps of *Mexico This Month* rest on the distortion and exaggeration that animate caricature, but they do so in ambivalent ways. A playful effect is clearly one outcome, although the series' post-touristic irony could be, and was in other instances in the magazine, misinterpreted. An article on archaeology in a later issue of *Mexico This Month*, like the 'Treasure Hunters' map discussed above, also featured amusing tips for readers on how to locate and access buried treasures, for, it claimed, 'almost any place in the Republic can be picked out as an ideal base for a prober of the past'. The article prompted a complaint to Brenner from the then director of the Museo Nacional de Antropología, Ignacio Bernal, who observed that 'our laws do not allow excavation unless undertaken by a professional archaeologist affiliated with a responsible institution. Anyone taking seriously the [article's] suggestions may end up in jail' (Brenner 1965). Contrary to what Bernal might have thought, in many ways *Mexico This Month* was, like much of the print media of its day, frequently *oficialista* in character, with plenty of material in its issues to support John Mraz's characterization of Mexico's contemporary illustrated magazines as eminently presidentialist in tone and outlook (2009: 173). The magazine ran regular features on the major achievements of each respective *sexenio* and in its early issues included a section called 'Quote worth remembering', which often came directly from the president's mouth. Given the circumstances of the magazine's launch, its 'diplomatic' objectives and generous state funding arrangements (to which I return in the next section), this perhaps comes as no surprise. Of more interest is another outcome of the cartographic affinity with caricature discussed here, which articulates a complex position with regard to the industry in which *Mexico This Month* was invested. The serialization of the Explorers' Maps hints at the impossibility and interminability of the very practice of mapping and the realization that 'the land never remains static for long, whatever the scientific claims to measure and map it accurately' (Brotton 2012: 334). Moreover, and consonant with Brotton's proposal of a 'cartography without progress', as invoked in this chapter's epigraph (words which are true of the fate of many a magazine), the Explorers' Maps of *Mexico This Month* attest to an aesthetic fusion of touristic and colonial images that might in fact serve oppositional purposes.

III

If certain maps in the Explorers' Maps series legitimized economic activity by thematizing it, albeit uneasily, Brenner's tribulations as editor of *Mexico This Month* over the seventeen years of its lifetime also rested largely and often urgently on the issue of capital. *Mexico This Month* had a complex funding structure: a small percentage of individual subscribers as well as contracts for subscriptions with private companies for the promotion of their services connected with Mexico, as for example, in the case of Humble Oil, who distributed the magazine at its travel information offices on the Mexican border. The magazine's financial security was underwritten, however, by a substantial state subsidy that ensured that the majority of its income derived from bulk 'controlled circulation'. Brenner was mindful of the implications of this for editorial independence, insisting in the magazine's pages and in various memoranda that: 'no publicamos unas gacetillas de ninguna especie, ni políticas ni comerciales … hemos optado por no comprometer jamás este precioso capital moral que se logra … siguiendo esta política editorial' [we don't publish sponsored advertising of any political or commercial kind … we have chosen never to compromise that precious moral capital gained by pursuing this editorial policy] (Brenner 1964). Notwithstanding, as mentioned above, the magazine was largely *oficialista* in tone, both for good and ill. While progressive on the question of Cuba, like many of her mainstream media counterparts, the magazine was largely acquiescent on other political issues of national significance, its tone suitably triumphalist during the 1968 Olympics, for example, though its pages fell silent on the Tlatelolco massacre. Nevertheless, a striking advertisement in the magazine's November 1968 issue, which was still devoted in large part to coverage of the Olympics and its legacy, seems significant in retrospect: an eye-catching announcement of an exhibition of the work of the Catalan artist and regular magazine contributor Bartoli called 'Extermination Camp' at the Juan Martin Gallery: '[his] drawings put down a lifetime of experience with the more violent political phenomena of our time' (14:9, 1968, 30). As we saw in the previous chapter, here the heterogeneous admixture of different types of (visual, textual, commercial, and editorial) material in the magazine not only 'competes for readers' attention' but can 'work together to create meaning' (Hammill and Smith 2015: 4).

Mexico This Month's subsidy, split between the Banco Nacional de Mexico and Nacional Financiera, and which speaks to the broader dependency of culture on the Mexican state, had aesthetic as well as material implications. The Banco de Mexico was the first to subsidize the magazine, buying 12,000 of its average 30,000 monthly copies on behalf of the Department of Tourism. These were then distributed to embassies, consulates, and tourist delegations in the US and beyond as well as to private enterprises in the tourism sector (Brenner boasted of subscriptions from 'remote' places 'such as India and the Isle of Wight', 2:4, 1956, 7). This was consonant with long-standing endeavours by the central bank, 'one of the most orthodox institutions of Mexican government', in the development of tourism in Mexico.[18] Nacional Financiera purchased a further 15,000 copies for general promotional purposes which were sent to press, libraries, airlines, travel agencies and universities.[19] The two subsidies covered the estimated $2 unit cost at the magazine's launch in 1955, with a further 30% discount—agreed by Loyo—on the purchase of paper from a US manufacturer then based in Mexico. Scarcely three years into operations, however, that discount was withdrawn, although increased commercial advertising revenues temporarily compensated for the loss. Brenner acknowledged that the magazine needed to be self-sufficient but lamented that advertising 'es difícil, ya que por lo general [en México] la publicidad en revistas se considera algo así como una propina, en vez de un justo pago por valores recibidos' [is difficult, since generally in Mexico magazine advertising is considered like a tip, rather than a fair payment for values received] (Brenner 1964). Notwithstanding, she saw its merit as an indicator of the magazine's independence, its commercial associations aligning it with the 'intereses reales económicos de la nación' [real economic interests of the nation] (Brenner 1964). In 1960 Brenner succeeded in renegotiating with Nacional Financiera to cover the (actual) cost price of $2.40 but not with the Banco de Mexico, which regarded the magazine a 'negocio particular' [private business]. From then on, notwithstanding a smaller package deal with Humble Oil and its regular individual subscribers, and with rising costs in printing and paper, the magazine was soon in severe financial straits.

Various measures were proposed and taken to tackle this deficit, including reducing staff and operating costs in addition to cutting issue length and the magazine's frequency. By 1962 *Mexico This Month* had halved its issue length from an average of thirty-two pages to sixteen. Brenner was then encouraged to buy paper, 'the single biggest expense in manufacturing a periodical' (Rubenstein 2010: 601), from PIPSA. Mexico did not produce much paper of her own and relied on imports largely from Canada and the United States, where the major suppliers were located, and like other commodities, paper's costs varied in response to the strength of the *peso* and other variables, including the Second World War, which made it scarce and expensive. The state-owned semi-official Productora e Importadora de Papel, S.A. (PIPSA) imported newsprint to Mexico duty free and supplied publishers with paper at cut-rate prices: in providing paper at a steady, low price, it made possible the operation or suspension of mainstream and marginal publications and became a powerful state tool to ensure the political compliance of the print media. In consequence, for most of the twentieth-century PRI hegemony, in a context in which the press historically has had 'complacent relations with state and market interests', the media were 'fully integrated into the structure of power' (Hallin 2000: 83).[20] Indeed, by the 1940s, PIPSA had so abused its powers that the owners of the largest newspapers in the capital 'were looking for a way around this situation' (Nilbo 1991: 351) and yet, as Rubenstein discloses, between 1940 and 1976, newspapers that were 'independent' of PIPSA 'never lasted more than a year' (Rubenstein 2010: 602). Brenner decried the PIPSA proposal and the paper's poor quality but relented, insisting that it be a 'medida transitoria' [temporary measure] to be used only in certain sections of the magazine. The results she said, writing in 1962, were wholly detrimental to the magazine's and thus too to Mexico's image abroad: 'nos mutila el aspecto y causa una malísma impresión en el extranjero' [it maims our appearance and causes a terrible impression abroad] (Brenner 1962). The aesthetic diminishment imposed by the change in paper was thus inimical to the principles of the magazine's foundation, as well as further destabilized its avowed editorial independence. Needless to say, Brenner's enthusiasm for using colour photography, to take advantage of 'Mexico's wealth of beauty in full colour', was also curtailed. 'Most countries', she observed pointedly, 'consider [colour photography] a necessity. However, since it will require about ten times our production costs even to begin to attempt it we can only aim at it as a valuable and necessary thing to do in the future' (Brenner 1960). The magazine's financial arrangements not only found expression in its modified appearance but also circumscribed plans for the expansion of its circulation and diversification.[21] Brenner's repeated efforts (from the late 1950s onwards) to find a suitable buyer for the magazine and to form an *empresa mixta*, with Mexican finance and US publishing expertise, came to nothing.[22] The withdrawal of the government subsidies, first from the Banco de Mexico in 1965, and, then, in December 1970 by Nacional Financiera, ultimately sealed *Mexico This Month*'s fate. The timing of the central bank's withdrawal seems particularly ironic, as it was precisely at that time that it wrote a plan calling for the aggressive marketing of Mexico to potential foreign tourists as an answer to the country's trade and development needs (Clancy 2001: 31).

In different ways, the fortunes of *Mexico This Month* and the visual language of its Explorers' Maps series both speak to a central ambivalence in the magazine's engagement with tourism over its seventeen-year lifetime. Indeed, the magazine's relationship with capital illuminates one of the many contradictions that emerge from a consideration of tourism in this context. Among these are the tensions relating to efforts to advertise the country's development and modernity through its diversity and history and to promote it as a vacation site to be consumed by US visitors seeking respite precisely from the very modernizing processes then being embraced in Mexico. The fundamental ambivalence, however, which underpinned the 'uneven and non-systematic' approach of the Mexican state to tourism across the post-war/Cold War period was about how to reconcile a desire for national sovereignty with market and geopolitical demands. Accordingly, the endorsement of President Ruiz Cortínez at the launch of *Mexico This Month* was eclipsed early on and most definitively by the central bank's retreat after the election of the more repressive

President Díaz Ordaz, who, like President López Mateos before him (1958–1964), wavered in his enthusiasm for tourism.[23] In essence, for all its efforts to promote development, modernity and the transnational flow of capital, *Mexico This Month*, though hampered by a certain degree of editorial and official protectionism, was hamstrung by domestic politics and the effects on its finance and production of a state-driven tourist industry which, still in its relative infancy, operated in fits and starts over the two decades of the magazine's operation. One terminal manifestation of this emerged in the late 1960s, when developers and investors started to consider the potential of the Yucatán coastline as a setting for a new beach resort. As Mayas flocked to the area seeking jobs, the 'tourist mecca' of Cancún started to take shape as the first hotels began to open to mostly North American tourists (Sherman 2010: 567). Such attempts to revive the Mexican 'miracle' in the 'Riviera Maya'—together with the development of *maquiladoras* in the country's border regions—began to stall even by the early 1970s, however, as the contradictions on which Mexico's postwar economic boom rested struggled to keep hold.

In this respect, as Clancy has observed, state reliance on tourism requires constant planning and promotional efforts: at national level this demands perennial newness. Brenner was cognizant of this. An episode documented in her correspondence, which speaks to that demand, provides a fitting yet chilling ending for this chapter's considerations, returning us to that central affiliation between revolution and tourism with which this book began. Revolution and tourism, as I suggested in Chapter 1, are each a source of the 'new'—experientially and conceptually—and this anecdote from Brenner's archive testifies to the deep tensions produced by their coupling. Brenner was committed to both: counting herself among 'las filas intelectuales de la Revolución' [the intellectual ranks of the Revolution], she was throughout her career a tireless advocate of tourism as a form of goodwill ambassadorship. Nevertheless, as *Mexico This Month* folded in 1971, it was clear to her that in Mexico revolution was no longer synonymous with the modern and that this was a threat to tourism. On 9 June 1971, she wrote to a newly elected President Luis Echeverría attributing the resurgence of an 'inquietante bajón del turismo' [disturbing sharp fall in tourism] to the bloody events in the second half of the Díaz Ordaz *sexenio* (the massacre of student demonstrators in the Plaza del Tlatelolco) with which Echeverría, as former Minister of Government whose remit included domestic security, was closely associated:

La imagen de México como país revolucionario ya no existe [en la prensa de allá]. Ha sido destruida por todo lo reporteado de Tlatelolco ... del país del heroico Zapata y el valiente Cárdenas nos hemos transformado al país de los sacrificios humanos.

[The image of Mexico as a revolutionary country no longer exists (in the press over there). It has been destroyed by all the reporting about Tlatelolco ... from the home of heroic Zapata and brave Cárdenas we've become the country of human sacrifice].

The delivery of Brenner's letter was delayed as a result of another homicide that 'had been carried out with orders from the top' (Sherman 2010: 564); what became known as the Corpus Christi massacre, which took place in Mexico City on 10 June 1971.[24] En route to deliver it, the courier had to take cover for safety during the violence, during which dozens of students were killed. In a second letter to the president's office on 11 June to account for the first's delay, Brenner was apparently unmoved by the demonstrators' plight. Rather, in a gesture which resounds implacably with the founding objectives of the magazine she edited for so long, if not with her own radical past, Brenner's paramount concern was that 'en el extranjero el resultado neto va a ser una impresión de confusión y peligro y va a hacer mucho daño para la entrada del turismo de verano' [abroad the net result will be an impression of confusion and danger and it will do a lot of damage to the start of the summer tourism season] (Brenner 1971).

Notes

1. In this respect, the following assertion by Carl Thomson (2011: 25) is suggestive: that 'insofar as they are artfully constructed representations of the world that are often ideologically charged and laden with larger cultural meanings ...one might plausibly include maps ... as a form of travel writing.'
2. Saragoza (2001: 104) claims that 'the mix of Acapulco's significance and Alemán's influence forced reconciliation of the "modern" tourism exemplified by beachside resorts with the heritage-based approach of the 1930s'.
3. For more on this see Anderson (1998).
4. Brenner insisted that the members of the magazine's founding committee, many of them business men, had such intimacy with the country, garnered through years of residency there, that they 'have developed a feeling almost as if its problems were like illness in the family, and its accomplishments, personal triumphs' (*Mexico This Month*, 1:1, 6).

5. See *Mexico This Month*, 1:2 (1955). For more on this see Cohn (2005).
6. See, respectively, *Mexico This Month*, 2:8 (August 1956); 9:5 (August 1963); 2:12 (December 1956).
7. Brenner's experiment with launching a mail order *rebozo* business was eventually hamstrung by irregularities in the postal service, an experience she equated with 'the Sorcerer's Apprentice carrying his buckets of water' (5:12, 1959, 7).
8. Patricia Okker claims that a rhetoric of intimacy—or 'sisterly editorial voice'—was a trademark of periodicals edited by and for women in the US in the nineteenth century. See Okker (1995: 23).
9. In the Anglophone world, for example, it was during this period that the Ordnance Survey of Great Britain started to make tourist maps for the leisure market, 'with evocative illustrated covers and in a convenient folded format'. Harper (2016: 149).
10. For more on branding in Latin America see Fehimović and Ogden (2018).
11. For more on how US advertisers tapped into Mexican nationalism during and after WWII, see Moreno (2003).
12. For a fascinating discussion of maps and money see also Brotton (2012: 260–293). On the use of the figure of the cornucopia as a trope in Mexico's visual culture, see Carrera (2011: 117).
13. The Casa de la Contratación used information from voyages to the Americas to modify and update maritime charts and also produced the *padrón general*, 'a master chart of the known world'. For more on this see Carrera (2011: 39).
14. Indeed, as the Paseo began to develop during the *Porfiriato* the city began to divide in two: the wealthy, including the American colony, in the west, while 'the eastern part of the city remained a place for the poor'. Boardman (2001: 48).
15. Garrigan shows how the history behind these statues reveals the critical tensions between patrimony and commerce, the very conditions the former was supposed to transcend. She illustrates, for example, how the statue to Columbus was, rather than 'inspired nationalism', in fact 'a compensatory gesture for a failed business transaction in which [Antonio] Escandón [the Mexican capitalist who had commissioned the monument] had been unable to fulfill his original obligation' (Garrigan 2012: 107, 118).
16. I have borrowed this useful phrase from James Martin (2011).
17. Brotton, in relation to the *Carte de Cassini*, 'the first modern map of a nation', concurs that 'any national survey [is] potentially endless' (2012: 334).
18. For example, when the National Trust for Tourist Infrastructure (INFRATUR) was created in 1969 it was administered within the central

bank, 'indicat[ing] that tourism promotion came in response to balance of payments pressures and was conceived of mainly as an export project' (Clancy 2001: 51).
19. Nacional Financiera was 'a credit institution which aided investment [in Mexico] by floating bonds and managing both public and private funds, including many of the major loans granted for public works' (Sherman 2010: 547).
20. PIPSA had the authority to provide its clients, both newspapers and journals, not only with their own supply but, indeed, with a surplus of paper which could then be sold at a profit to buyers without the requisite governmental approval, an unofficial income that 'in some cases accounted for up to 40% of a newspaper's income'. See Cohn (2005: 174).
21. These included a convention service and a multi-media package for schools, as well as other teaching materials for Chicano programmes in the US.
22. Brenner attempted to convene an 'empresa mixta' with capital investment from Mexico, and editorial and production talent from the US. In 1971, she also investigated the possibility of the Holiday Inn using *Mexico This Month* in its promotional material specifically in the Holiday Inn magazine.
23. Both presidents were hesitant to promote tourism more strongly, says Clancy, which resulted from problems with border tourism. Coastal tourism, as a result, was neglected at this time. But the withdrawal of the central bank might also have to do with the state's retreat from a more aggressive stance as entrepreneur and banker to more of a back seat as private investment began to increase during this period.
24. At a student demonstration, a crowd of right-wing thugs set upon unarmed protesters with knives and light weapons, killing two or three dozen of them, as police stood and watched.

References

Anderson, Mark C. 1998. 'What's to Be Done with 'Em?' Images of Mexican Cultural Backwardness, Racial Limitations, and Moral Decrepitude in the United States Press 1913–1915.' *Mexican Studies/Estudios Mexicanos* 14 (1): 23–70.

Boardman, Andrea. 2001. *Destination Mexico, 'A Foreign Land a Step Away': US Tourism to Mexico 1880s–1950s.* Dallas: Southern Methodist University.

Brenner, Anita.1932. *Your Mexican Holiday.* New York: Putnams.

———. 1955. 'Closing Speech to the Congress of Inter-American Studies.' University of Florida, December, *Anita Brenner Papers* 16:8.

———. 1959. Anon. to Anita Brenner, 12 June, n.p. *Anita Brenner Papers* 83:9.

———. 1960. Memorandum on Tourist Travel. *Anita Brenner Papers* 108:5.
———. 1962. Memorandum. 24 de abril. *Anita Brenner Papers* 108:5.
———. 1964. Memo on Tourist Travel. *Anita Brenner Papers* 108:5.
———. 1965. Ignacio Bernal to Anita Brenner, 9 September. *Anita Brenner Papers* 83:1.
———. 1967. Anita Brenner to Xerox, 25 October. *Anita Brenner Papers* 97:3.
———. 1971. Anita Brenner to Fausto Zapata Loredo, Subsecretaria de la Presidencia, 11 June. *Anita Brenner Papers* 96:4.
———. n.d. Memorandum, *Anita Brenner Papers* 96:5.
Brotton, Jerry. 2012. *A History of the World in Twelve Maps.* London: Penguin.
Carrera, Magalí. 2011. *Travelling from New Spain to Mexico: Mapping Practices of 19th-Century Mexico.* Durham: Duke University Press.
Clancy, Michael. 2001. *Exporting Paradise: Tourism and Development in Mexico* Amsterdam: Pergamon.
Cohn, Deborah. 2005. 'The Mexican Intelligentsia, 1950–1968: Cosmopolitanism, National Identity, and the State'. *Mexican Studies/Estudios Mexicanos* 21 (1): 141–182.
Corner, James. 1999. 'The Agency of Mapping: Speculation, Critique and Invention.' In *Mappings*, edited by Denis Cosgrove, 213–252. London: Reaktion.
Cosgrove, Denis. 1999. 'Introduction: Mapping Meaning.' In *Mappings*, edited by Denis Cosgrove, 1–23. London: Reaktion.
Craib, Raymond. 2004. *Cartographic Mexico: A History of State Fixations and Fugitive Landscapes.* Durham: Duke University Press.
———. 2011. 'Historical Geographies.' In *Mapping Latin America: A Cartographic Reader*, edited by Jordana Dym and Karl Offen, 153–158. Chicago: University of Chicago Press.
de Certeau, Michel. 1984. *The Practice of Everyday Life.* Berkeley: University of California Press.
Dwyer, Owen J. 2003. 'Memory on the Margins: Alabama's Civil Rights Journey as a Memorial Text.' In *Mapping Tourism*, edited by Stephen P. Hanna and Vincent J. del Casino Jr., 28–50. Minneapolis: University of Minnesota Press.
Fehimović, Dunja, and Rebecca Ogden, eds. 2018. *Branding Latin America: Strategies, Aims, Resistance.* Lanham: Lexington Books.
Garrigan, Shelley E. 2012. *Collecting Mexico: Museums, Monuments, and the Creation of National Identity.* Minneapolis: University of Minnesota Press.
Gillingham, Paul, and Benjamin T. Smith, eds. 2014. *Dictablanda: Politics, Work, and Culture in Mexico, 1938–1968.* Durham: Duke University Press.
Glusker, Susannah Joel. 1998. *Anita Brenner: A Mind of Her Own.* Austin: University of Texas Press.
Hallin, Daniel C. 2000. 'Media, Political Powers and Democratization in Mexico.' In *De-Westernising Media Studies*, edited by J. Curran and M.-J. Park, 85–97. London and New York: Routledge.

Hammill, Faye, and Michelle Smith. 2015. *Magazines, Travel and Middlebrow Culture: Canadian Periodicals in English and French 1925–1960*. Liverpool: Liverpool University Press.
Hammill, Faye, Paul Hjartarson, and Hannah McGregor. 2015. 'Introducing Magazines and/as Media: The Aesthetics and Politics of Serial Form.' *ESC: English Studies in Canada* 41 (1): 1–18.
Hanna, Stephen P., and Vincent J. del Casino Jr., eds. 2003. *Mapping Tourism*. Minneapolis: University of Minnesota Press.
Harley, J. B., and David Woodward. 1992. *History of Cartography*. Vol. I. Chicago: University of Chicago Press.
Harmon, Katharine. 2009. *The Map as Art: Contemporary Artists Explore Cartography*. New York: Princeton Architectural Press.
Harper, Tom. 2016. *Maps and the Twentieth Century*. London: British Library.
Johns, Michael. 1997. *The City of Mexico in the Age of Díaz*. Austin: University of Texas Press.
Martin, James. 2011. 'Mapping an Empire: Tourist Cartographies of the Caribbean in the Early 20th Century.' *Early Popular Visual Culture* 9 (1): 1–14.
McClintock, Anne. 1995. *Imperial Leather: Race, Gender and Sexuality in the Colonial Contest*. New York: Routledge.
Monsivais, Carlos. 2010. 'Introduction: Anita Brenner: The (Multiple) Story of Origins.' In *Avant Garde Art and Artists in Mexico: Anita Brenner's Journals of the Roaring Twenties and Thirties*, edited by Susannah Joel Glusker, xi–xxiv. Austin: University of Texas Press.
Moreno, Julio. 2003. *Yankee Don't Go Home! Mexican Nationalism, American Business Culture, and the Shaping of Modern Mexico, 1920–1950*. Chapel Hill: University of North Carolina Press.
Mraz, John. 2009. *Looking for Mexico: Modern Visual Culture and National Identity*. Durham: Duke University Press.
Nilbo, Stephen R. 1991. *Mexico in the 1940s: Modernity, Politics, and Corruption*. Wilmington: Scholarly Resources.
Okker, Patricia. 1995. *Our Sister Editors: Sarah J. Hale and the Tradition of Nineteenth-Century Woman Editors*. Athens: University of Georgia Press.
Padrón, Ricardo. 2004. *The Spacious Word: Cartography, Literature and Early Modern Spain*. Chicago: University of Chicago Press.
Radcliffe, Sarah A. 2011. 'Representing the Nation.' In *Mapping Latin America: A Cartographic Reader*, edited by Jordana Dym and Karl Offen, 207–210. Chicago: University of Chicago Press.
Rubenstein, Anne. 2010. 'Mass Media and Popular Culture in the Postrevolutionary Era.' In *The Oxford History of Mexico*, edited by William H. Beezley and Michael C. Meyer, 598–634. New York: Oxford University Press.
Ryan, Simon. 1994. 'Inscribing the Emptiness: Cartography, Exploration and the Construction of Australia.' In *De-Scribing Empire: Postcolonialism and Textuality*, edited by Chris Tiffin and Alan Lawson, 126–127. London: Routledge.

Salvatore, Ricardo. 1998. 'The Enterprise of Knowledge: Representational Machines of Informal Empire'. In *Close Encounters of Empire: Writing the Cultural History of U.S.-Latin American Relations*, edited by Gilbert Joseph, Catherine Le Grand, and Ricardo Salvatore, 69–104. Durham: Duke University Press.

Saragoza, Alex. 2001. 'The Selling of Mexico: Tourism and the State, 1929–1952.' In *Fragments of a Golden Age: The Politics of Culture in Mexico Since 1940*, edited by Gilbert Joseph, Anne Rubenstein, and Eric Zolov, 91–115. Durham: Duke University Press.

Sherman, John. 2010. 'The Mexican "Miracle" and its Collapse.' In *The Oxford History of Mexico*, edited by William Beezly and Michael C. Meyer, 537–568. Oxford: Oxford University Press.

Shields, Rob. 2003. 'Political Tourism: Mapping Memory and the Future of Quebec City.' In *Mapping Tourism*, edited by Stephen P. Hanna and Vincent J. Del Casino Jr., 1–27. Minneapolis: University of Minnesota Press.

Tenorio Trillo, Mauricio. 2010. 'El peso de una imagen: México.' In *México ilustrado: libros, revistas y carteles 1920–1950*, edited by Salvador Albiñana, 20. Mexico: Editorial RM.

———. 2012. *I Speak of the City: Mexico at the Turn of the 20th Century (1880–1940)*. Chicago: University of Chicago Press.

Thompson, Carl. 2011. *Travel Writing*. Oxford and New York: Routledge.

Urry, John. 2002. *The Tourist Gaze*, 2nd ed. London: Sage.

Woods, Richard D. 1990. 'Anita Brenner: Cultural Mediator for Mexico.' *Studies in Latin American Popular Culture* 9: 209.

Open Access This chapter is licensed under the terms of the Creative Commons Attribution 4.0 International License (http://creativecommons.org/licenses/by/4.0/), which permits use, sharing, adaptation, distribution and reproduction in any medium or format, as long as you give appropriate credit to the original author(s) and the source, provide a link to the Creative Commons license and indicate if changes were made.

The images or other third party material in this chapter are included in the chapter's Creative Commons license, unless indicated otherwise in a credit line to the material. If material is not included in the chapter's Creative Commons license and your intended use is not permitted by statutory regulation or exceeds the permitted use, you will need to obtain permission directly from the copyright holder.

CHAPTER 5

Conclusion

Abstract By way of conclusion to the preceding arguments, this chapter, drawing on ideas from the new formalism and media studies history, pursues the implications of the magazines' rhythm and serialization with respect to theories of nation-building in the context of post-revolutionary Mexico. In its summation of the ramifications of the book's findings, it also returns to the suggestive idea of archive, first rehearsed in Chapter 1, to consider the concept's material and epistemological value for this particular object of study.

Keywords Magazines · Mobility · Serialization · Rhythm · Modernity · Archive

In the nineteenth century, museums and monuments represented mass visual commemorations of patrimony, in which 'a fixed repertory of traditions [was] condensed into objects'. In the decades following Revolution, when only then '[the reimagining of the nation] c[a]me to include non-elites' (Tenorio Trillo 1996: 8, 1) illustrated transnational magazines such as *Mexican Folkways* and *Mexico This Month*, I suggest, fulfilled an analogous, yet distinct function. Insofar as they too shaped and became a constitutive part of the very spaces they imagined, they operated as a potentially democratic, though volatile, modern showcase of culture. Discrete historical circumstances in Mexico are critical here:

during the first half of the twentieth century, as Néstor García Canclini has pointed out, 'the documentation and diffusion of patrimony [in Mexico] was done through *temporary and travelling exhibits*, cultural missions, and muralism' (my emphasis) rather than in more durable forms of 'exhibition in museums of a definitively established national culture' (1995: 117). Indeed, while short-lived newspapers had run throughout the *Porfiriato* and during the Revolution, it was during the 1920s, as I described in the Introduction, that cultural and political journals proliferated in Mexico 'as independent or government projects' (Lear 2017: 87). This was, I contend, a primary 'period of periodicals' (an epithet I borrow from Deborah Cohn's characterization of Mexico's mid-century decades, 2005: 165), when cheap and rapidly produced print, though ephemeral, had significant advantages over other media forms then being deployed, offering greater immediacy of diffusion as well as 'greater autonomy from state patronage compared to murals painted on the walls of public buildings' (Lear 2017: 10–11). The very 'mobility' of periodicals, their responsiveness and serialization throw into further relief those fixed, permanent sites of monuments, museums, and (most, if not all) murals, which in turn encouraged particular forms of viewing and touring practices. Periodicals circulated among a variety of audiences (subscribers, casual readers, a pass-along readership) in different locations, at different times, and in potentially myriad ways. As such, it is not just that their editors 'synchronize[d] cultural production to the vertiginous speed of an incipient modernity' (Gallo 2005: 1), as Rubén Gallo proposes in *Mexican Modernity* of the new media revolutionaries of the 1920s and 1930s; in fact, those magazines enunciated its mood, pace, and 'logic'.

For the natural state of being of magazines, media historian Mark W. Turner proposes, is 'change and movement', attributes that, for Turner, mean that the media provides the very rhythm of modernity (Turner 2002: 184). In establishing the pattern of everyday life, competing inordinate periodical titles enunciate diverse subject matter and different temporalities according to their publication schedules: quarterliness, weekliness, dailiness. Anita Brenner fully understood the calendrical value of magazines and its auxiliary social capital (that is, the potential of rhythmic form to do 'serious political work', Levine 2015: 49): she proposed that a ritual monthly travel magazine like *Mexico This Month* was imperative in the new Republic, for it was 'cosa de cajón en todo país moderno' [*de rigueur* in every modern country] (Brenner 1965).

Between its covers, *Mexico This Month* chronicled seasonal patterns of Mexico's fiestas, with regular coverage and an annual pull-out calendar of national and local celebrations such as the September Grito, the November Day of the Dead and Lunes de cerro in Oaxaca. It also measured the metre of political processes; publishing details of the president's annual address to Congress, for example, while its features on the presidential rotation each *sexenio* were a staple in the magazine's seventeen-year lifespan. *Mexican Folkways*, though more discontinuous in publication and in parsing folklore in quite the same formats as the later magazine, was replete with features on regional 'costumbres y fiestas' or on indigenous rituals of courtship, marriage, and burial, as well as song scores from across the Republic. Both magazines marked tempo in another fashion by advertising special Christmas gift issues as well as anniversary offers celebrating the journals' own duration. In this respect, notwithstanding the latent power of rhythm to control and subjugate, the periodicity of magazines has a generative function, producing a sense of 'communal solidarity' and that 'simultaneity' Benedict Anderson associates with nationhood; an understanding of the pulse—as well as the terrain—of national experience and belonging.

Nevertheless, in the media landscape, as Turner reminds us, there is no one single rhythm, but always cacophony and asynchrony: 'The present is the past here and it is the future too', he writes, 'if we remember the next issue awaits us' (2002: 192). On one level, both magazines' interrupted and reconfigured serialization (the change from bi-monthly to quarterly publication in the case of *Folkways*, for instance) within the broader context of multiple periodical titles speak to multiple patternings of time that contradict or compete with one another. This is not necessarily a purely 'modern' phenomenon, for separations between past, present, and future were/are indistinguishable to many of Mexico's indigenous peoples, as they were to intellectuals like Carlos Fuentes (1972). Yet, readers and subscribers of magazines such as *Folkways* and *Mexico This Month* frequently experienced a particular expression of 'untimeliness'. This is thematized and ironized in the following not untypical letter in the September 1958 issue of *Mexico This Month*, which spotlights the capacity for rhythmic repetitions to be broken. Fittingly, it construes that atemporality as a colonial legacy, resting on the historical imprecision of route-finding (Fig. 5.1).

Here the idea of simultaneity across space, central to Anderson's thesis on nationhood, breaks down: as readers (as much as the editors) of these

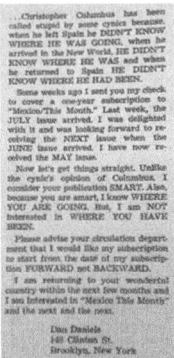

Fig. 5.1 Reader's letter, *Mexico This Month*

transnational titles discern the gap between 'periphery' and 'centre' they also register what Trish Loughran evocatively describes as the 'materialist corollary' of print culture as a great 'unifier': that is, 'a sense of scatteredness, or dispersion-across-space' (2007: 11).

The temporal disjunctions in the advertising and cartographic images identified in previous chapters speak to other breaches in temporality and periodization on and off the pages of these magazines. In *Mexican Folkways*, the Hotel Genève's forward-looking architectural frame and futuristic, vacant vestibule (both akin to the line of modernist photography of the period and resonant of the expectations of national elites who then valued tourism for the modernity it could bring about in terms of capital) rub up against the colonial nostalgia of its interior furnishings, décor, and Porfirian associations. At a time when the fidelity and congruity of the 'new' technology of photography were readily embraced, El Buen Tono's anachronistic hand-drawn advertisements correlate their products with an economy of making and authenticity associated with 'timeless' traditions documented elsewhere in *Folkways*, camouflaging not only the products' manufacturing processes but also the company's own historical complicity in the extinction of artisan cigarette production in Mexico. In *Mexico This Month*, the Explorers' Maps series articulates an arresting dialectic between the pre-modern function of the map as history book (expressed, *inter alia*, in an iconographic vocabulary, tour describers, and use of cartouches) and a keen post-touristic irony, which also potentially jeopardizes the magazine's founding initiatives. Those maps' fusion of the modern and colonial, as well as their repetition and number over the series' four-year duration, hints at the impossibility of mapping Mexico at all, evoking Magalí Carrera's characterization of cartography as 'an endless overwriting that is never complete' (2011: 9). On one level, such asynchrony attests to the 'cultures in conflict' that define (not only postrevolutionary) Mexico, as Anne Rubenstein lucidly remarks;

> "Tradition" did not precede "modernity" any more than modernity displaced tradition. Each required the other. And both were aspects of a single national culture that was developing throughout this period. (1998: 6, 42)

On another level, it further problematizes the neat association between a common print culture and the formation of a shared national consciousness. In a context of precarious and fitful sources of funding, such 'untimely' aesthetic qualities together with temporal lags in these periodicals' publication and distribution all suggest that the work of the media in consolidating a modern Republic as a singular bounded whole was much more complex, processual (and 'virtual') in post-revolutionary reality than in theory. Indeed, as Loughran writes of a germane context: 'Nations are in fact always incomplete, cross-generational, noninevitable, and *ongoing* enterprises' (Loughran 2007: xviii, original emphasis).

* * * *

In his recent book *Culture and Revolution*, Horacio Legrás laments that the archive of sources on Mexico's revolutionary period has now expanded to the degree that it 'is 'beyond control or description' 'exceed[ing] the ability of any researcher to master [it]' (2017: 2). To want to situate magazines such as *Mexican Folkways* and *Mexico This Month* within a repository of the post-revolutionary period that is equally incommensurable might seem a foolhardy endeavour. Yet such an endeavour warrants the risk in part precisely because of these magazines' own aspirations as archival collections. If we understand the latter to be, in Geoffrey Yeo's words, 'a persistent representation of activities created by participants or observers of those activities, or by their authorized proxies' (Yeo 2007: 337), *Mexican Folkways* and *Mexico This Month* very much operated in those terms. In regularly recording and relaying knowledge about Mexico north/south, with posterity in mind, they also functioned according to Derrida's depiction of the archive, as 'a pledge … a token of the future' (Derrida 1995: 18). To be sure, as I discussed in Chapter 1, such magazines pose particular methodological challenges, in part because of those very qualities shared with many an archive or archival impulse, namely their scope, size, ambition, and persistence. Their total number of pages over several years or decades can be vast, such that in the case of *Mexico This Month* at least, its entire seventeen-years'-worth of monthly content poses problems of apprehension and command of the kind identified by Legrás. A comprehensive and exhaustive engagement with it all would indeed require a collaborative team of researchers of the like of Franco Moretti's and Matthew Jocker's Stanford Literary Lab, the work of which would benefit from digital tools to map the 'messy' yet valuable data between and beyond its covers. The publication of Ralph Boggs's valuable annotated bibliography and index of the content of *Mexican Folkways* (1945) arguably anticipated the kind of work that even 'simple' digital applications like Neatline now make possible in visual shorthand. Other methodological challenges arise in part because of the ways in which magazines have been preserved as sources. Library and archival holdings are often incomplete or fail to preserve the periodicals in their original published formats. In many ways, this in itself provides a rationale for their digitization, although digital avatars are not equivalents of their physical forms and cannot capture significant features of the magazine as a material object, including, for example, size, texture, paper quality or weight. Moreover, these magazines' transnational authorship, content, and concomitant copyright issues might also hinder such an exercise. That is not a reason to not pursue such projects or other kinds of research on these magazines, however: the task is to find ways in which the digital and the analogue, distant and close reading, as well as individual and collaborative research, can be brought together for productive ends.

That, to recall the words of Carlos Monsivais one final time, the Revolution in Mexico 'was too many things at the same time' (Monsivais 2010: xi) is less a phenomenon to regret, I suggest, than an invitation to be alert to the coexistence and ramifications of the coincidence of cultures, epochs, and aesthetics as the Republic's geography and identity, with the aid of tourism, started to find expression. In the decades after Revolution, in their number, composition and often-interrupted serialization, magazines keenly articulated and documented that cadence of unseasonable-ness and surfeit. Indeed, they kindle precisely the kind of 'postmodern' contribution to Mexico's past as advocated by García Canclini, an approach, he avers, that 'reveals the constructed and staged character of all tradition, including that of modernity' (1995: 143). Moreover, if that post-revolutionary period was volatile, its repository of sources is likewise subject to change rather than stasis, for as Tom Nesmith reminds us, 'rather than being rendered inert in archives, records continually evolve. If they are to be preserved, they must change' (2002: 31). This is what Gabriella Nouzeilles refers to as the archival paradox, its 'hesitation between inscription and itinerancy' (2013: 41). Although as editors and 'archivists' of Mexican culture and traditions, Frances Toor and Anita Brenner were custodians of the material published between the covers of *Mexican Folkways* and *Mexico This Month*, scholars of such magazines (particularly those that are undigitized) perform a comparable custodianship in that ongoing dialectical process. For, as with the archivist's position, there is 'a type of authoring or [co]creating of the archival record' (Nesmith 2002: 32) at stake in the dynamic (re)construction, analysis, and interpretation of magazines as still 'living' artefacts and a concomitant responsibility in the mediation and dissemination of the knowledge available within them. In this regard, I take seriously DiCenzo's and others' emphasis on the tasks bestowed on researchers of periodicals, as what she calls 'history makers' (DiCenzo 2015: 32). I may of course stand accused of having crudely excavated details from *Mexican Folkways* and *Mexico This Month* for the purposes of this exploratory book—for it is true that there is more to be said about them than has been covered in these pages. Nevertheless, I have regarded my preliminary but fundamental task here to be to mediate these magazines' inaccessibility, be it temporal, cultural or material (as they are stored in archives some three thousand miles away from where I write) and, for the first time, to convey, navigate, and interrogate something of what is at stake in their complexity, diversity, and resonance. Writing this in the summer of 2018 when border tensions between Mexico and the United States resound with alarming echoes of early twentieth-century fascism, these magazines not only offer an instructive reminder of forms of transnational cooperation that test absolutist boundaries between 'foreign' and 'national' but also recall a time when journeys across the border were cast in terms of international public diplomacy.

References

Boggs, Ralph Steele. 1945. *Bibliografía completa, clasificada y comentada de los artículos de Mexican Folkways, con índice*. Mexico City: Instituto Panamericano de Geografía e Historia.

Brenner, Anita. 1965. *Memorandum*. Spring: n.p. *Anita Brenner Papers* 96:5.

Carrera, Magalí. 2011. *Travelling from New Spain to Mexico: Mapping Practices of Nineteenth-Century Mexico*. Durham: Duke University Press.

Cohn, Deborah. 2005. 'The Mexican Intelligentsia, 1950–1968: Cosmopolitanism, National Identity, and the State.' *Mexican Studies/Estudios Mexicanos* 21 (1): 141–182.

Derrida, Jacques. 1995. *Archive Fever: A Freudian Impression*. Chicago and London: University of Chicago Press.

DiCenzo, Maria. 2015. 'Remediating the Past: Doing "Periodical Studies" in the Digital Era.' *ESC: English Studies in Canada* 41 (1): 19–39.

Fuentes, Carlos. 1972. *Tiempo mexicano*. Mexico: Joaquín Mortiz.

Gallo, Rubén. 2005. *Mexican Modernity: The Avant-Garde and the Technological Revolution*. Cambridge: MIT Press.

García Canclini, Nestor. 1995. *Hybrid Cultures: Strategies for Entering and Leaving Modernity*. Translated by Christopher L. Chiappari and Silvia L. López. Minneapolis and London: University of Minnesota Press.

Lear, John. 2017. *Picturing the Proletariat: Artists and Labor in Revolutionary Mexico 1908–1940*. Austin: University of Texas Press.

Legrás, Horacio. 2017. *Culture and Revolution: Violence, Memory, and the Making of Modern Mexico*. Austin: University of Texas Press.

Levine, Caroline. 2015. *Forms: Whole, Rhythm, Hierarchy, Network*. Princeton: Princeton University Press.

Loughran, Trish. 2007. *The Republic in Print: Print Culture in the Age of U.S. Nation-Building, 1770–1870*. New York: Columbia University Press.

Monsivais, Carlos. 2010. 'Introduction: Anita Brenner: The (Multiple) Story of Origins.' In *Avant Garde Art and Artists in Mexico: Anita Brenner's Journals of the Roaring Twenties and Thirties*, edited by Susannah Joel Glusker, xi–xxiv. Austin: University of Texas Press.

Nesmith, Tom. 2002. 'Seeing Archives: Postmodernism and the Changing Intellectual Place of Archives.' *The American Archivist* 65 (1): 24–41.

Nouzeilles, Gabriella. 2013. 'The archival paradox.' In *The Itinerant Languages of Photography*, edited by Eduardo Cadava and Gabriella Nouzeilles, 38–53. Princeton, NJ: Princeton University Art Museum.

Rubenstein, Anne. 1998. *Bad Language, Naked Ladies, and Other Threats to the Nation: A Political History of Comic Books in Mexico*. Durham: Duke University Press.

Tenorio Trillo, Mauricio. 1996. *Mexico at the World's Fairs: Crafting a Modern Nation*. Berkeley and London: University of California Press.

Turner, Mark W. 2002. 'Periodical Time in the Nineteenth Century.' *Media History* 8 (2): 183–196.

Yeo, Geoffrey. 2007. 'Concepts of Record (1): Evidence, Information, and Persistent Representations.' *The American Archivist* 70 (2): 315–343.

Open Access This chapter is licensed under the terms of the Creative Commons Attribution 4.0 International License (http://creativecommons.org/licenses/by/4.0/), which permits use, sharing, adaptation, distribution and reproduction in any medium or format, as long as you give appropriate credit to the original author(s) and the source, provide a link to the Creative Commons license and indicate if changes were made.

The images or other third party material in this chapter are included in the chapter's Creative Commons license, unless indicated otherwise in a credit line to the material. If material is not included in the chapter's Creative Commons license and your intended use is not permitted by statutory regulation or exceeds the permitted use, you will need to obtain permission directly from the copyright holder.

Index

A
Advertising, 26, 29, 31, 39, 53–56, 60, 62, 63, 64–76, 79–81, 92, 95, 97, 99, 117, 129, 130
  of cigarettes, 77–79
  of hotels, 72–76
Alemán, Miguel, 22, 47, 94, 121
Anderson, Benedict, 1, 8–9, 129
  critique of, 13
Archive, 35, 36, 38, 55, 59, 81, 131, 133
  'archive entrepreneurs', 32, 46
Atlantic Monthly, 2

B
Boas, Franz, 33, 47, 57
Brenner, Anita, 1–4, 8, 12, 31, 32, 35, 36, 40, 47, 58, 73, 85, 100–102, 116–119, 120–122, 128, 133
Buelna, Alejandro, 3
Buen Tono, El, 12, 55, 72, 77–79, 85

C
Capital, 13, 22, 24, 45, 75, 80, 99, 122, 123, 130
Cárdenas, Lázaro, 94, 121
Cartography. *See* Maps
Commerce, 10, 54, 56, 62, 92, 122
Conquest, 93, 113, 114
Consumers/consumerism, 12, 55, 64, 66, 68–70, 77, 100, 101
Contemporáneos, 6, 37
Crisol, 6
Cuba, 19–20, 22–23, 27, 78, 79

D
Democracy, 2, 63, 64, 100
Díaz Ordaz, Gustavo, 120
Díaz, Porfirio, 63, 78, 79
  Porfiriato, 12, 56, 58, 63, 64, 75, 78–80, 94, 108, 122, 128, 130
Diplomacy, 7, 96, 101, 133

E
Echeverría, Luis, 120

138   INDEX

Editors. *See* Magazines
El libro y el pueblo, 6
El Machete, 6
El Maestro, 6
Excelsior, 2, 4

F
Forma: Revista de artes plásticas, 6
Fortune, 2

G
García Canclini, Néstor, 1, 9, 81, 132
Garrigan, Shelley, 9, 12, 55, 80, 122
Gore, Thomas, 73, 79

H
Hanna, Stephen P., 12, 93, 103–104
Hawley, Guillermo, 3
Holiday, 1–5, 34, 37, 47, 97
Horizonte, 6
Hotels, 12, 55, 65, 77, 120
 Hotel Genève, 72–76
 San Angel Inn, 76
 symbolic relationship to nation, 72

L
Life, 13, 98
López Mateos, Adolfo, 102, 120
López, Rick, 7, 56, 59–60

M
Mademoiselle, 2
Magazines, *passim*
 circulation, 8, 71, 72, 92, 105, 116, 119
 distribution, 11, 97, 131

editors, 3, 4, 7, 59, 61, 77, 81, 92, 105, 116, 119, 133
 'little magazine', 6, 54, 61, 65, 72
 readers, 2, 7, 59, 61, 66, 72, 73, 77, 81, 85, 98–100, 104, 105, 109, 111, 113, 117, 129
 tone, 4, 5, 71, 98, 102, 116, 117
Maps, 9, 11, 12, 76, 99, 102–116, 119
 and caricature, 107, 115, 116
 tourism maps, 103, 110
Mexican Folkways, 4, 7–8, 10, 11, 30, 33, 35, 36, 40–44, 54, 55, 56–65, 65–82, 98, 127, 129–133
Mexican Life: Mexico's Monthly Review, 7
Mexican World: Voice of Latin America, 7
Mexico, *passim*
 counter-revolution, 9, 10
 revolution, 2, 4, 5, 8, 10, 12, 55, 59, 61, 63, 77, 80, 81, 94, 120, 132
México moderno, 72
Mexico This Month, 4, 5, 7, 10, 12, 30, 31, 33, 35, 40, 42, 43, 92, 94–102, 103–119, 122, 123, 127–133
Modotti, Tina, 36, 62
Monsivais, Carlos, 8, 96, 132

N
Nationalism, 6, 8–10, 12, 57, 64, 84, 109, 122
Nationhood. *See* Anderson, Benedict
Nation, The, 2
New York Evening Post, 2
The New Yorker, 92
New York Times Sunday Magazine, The, 2

O
Orozco, José Clemente, 7, 56, 98

P
Paper, 11, 77, 107, 117
  Productora e importadora de papel, S.A. (PIPSA), 118, 123
Periodical studies, 11, 54
  methodological debates, 11, 54, 56, 81
  periodical codes, 37, 93
Photography, 64, 66, 71, 74–76
Porfiriato. See Díaz, Porfirio

R
Revista Crom, 6
Revista de revistas, 72
Revista musical de México, 72
Rivera, Diego, 7, 56, 59, 60, 62, 82, 98
Ruíz Cortínez, Adolfo, 96, 119

S
Siempre!, 98

T
Tenorio Trillo, Mauricio, 8, 10, 75, 85, 108, 109, 114, 127
Thomson, Krista, 27

tropicalisation, 75
Tlatelolco massacre, 117, 120
Toor, Frances, 5, 7, 56–61, 77, 81, 98, 133
Tourism, 3–11, 13, 18–27, 28, 32, 34, 35, 44, 53–55, 66, 72, 75, 82, 93, 94–96, 98, 99, 101–103, 115, 117, 121, 130, 132
  tourist/traveller dichotomy, 2, 13, 20, 21

U
Ulises, 6
United State, 2, 7, 24, 32, 43, 61, 79, 95, 100

V
Vincent J. del Casino, 13, 93, 103–104
Visual culture, 7, 8, 11, 56, 62, 66, 71, 81

W
Weston, Edward, 62, 65

The manufacturer's authorised representative in the EU is Springer Nature Customer Service Centre GmbH, Europaplatz 3, 69115 Heidelberg, Germany. If you have any concerns regarding our products, please contact ProductSafety@springernature.com

Printed and bound by CPI Group (UK) Ltd, Croydon, CR0 4YY

23/03/2026

02076401-0007